ISBN 978-1-331-14272-0
PIBN 10149939

" 'Wayne aimed and fired one of the field pieces himself.' "

[PAGE 71]

THE HERO OF STONY POINT

ANTHONY WAYNE

BY

JAMES BARNES

AUTHOR OF "RIFLE AND CARAVAN," "GIANT OF THREE WARS," "THE HERO
OF ERIE," ETC.

ILLUSTRATED BY

T. DE THULSTRUP

D. APPLETON AND COMPANY
NEW YORK   LONDON
1916

CONTENTS

CONTENTS

LIST OF ILLUSTRATIONS

THE HERO
OF STONY POINT

CHAPTER I

SCHOOL DAYS AT CHESTER—THE FIGHTING DUNCE

A SMALL boy of eleven sat on the end of a newly felled log in a clearing of the Chester woods. He was a sturdily built, thickset youngster whose appearance would have little suggested the occupation at which we find him. With compressed lips and a deal of squinting he was trying to force through the eye of a much too small needle the end of a much too large thread. After many trials, pursued with an infinite patience, he succeeded. On the log beside him lay two strips of red cloth. Tucked into the edge of his small three-cornered hat, was a bundle of turkey feathers that only a half an hour before had been proudly spread by the old gobbler, who, panting and much disheveled, was hiding in an angle of the chicken yard fence a few rods away. The boy had had his eyes on the tail feathers for many a long day and had waited for the moment when, without fear of interference, he could despoil the old gobbler of his principal adornment.

With remarkable skill the boy began to sew the feathers between the strips of red cloth, and having basted them in so they stood firmly upright, he measured the band round his head, sewed the two ends together and, going down to a pool in the brook, looked at his reflection with all the self-satisfaction of a Narcissus. Going back to the log where he had left his coat and hat, he discovered that there was a rent in his coat sleeve; sitting down, he mended it neatly before putting it on.

Although incongruous, the Indian-like decoration became the boy's face better than the old three-cornered hat, for he had the high cheek bone, the deep-set eyes of the red man, and his little hawk-like features needed but to be a shade or two darker than the coat of tan that covered them, to make him, to all appearances, a juvenile member of the Seven Nations.

Carrying his hat under his arm, he walked along the path through the blackberry bushes, heading past the chicken yard where the hen turkeys had not yet settled down from the excitement they had undergone in witnessing the struggle and discomfiture of their lord and master. Reaching a barn and stable made of rough hewn logs, the boy bent down and, lifting aside an old barrel-head, disclosed a hiding-place in the stone foundation. It was here that he kept the things most near and dear to him; a bow whittled out of a hickory limb, a bundle of cleverly made arrows, and an actual Indian tomahawk that had been given to him by a man who had made a trading trip out into the great western forests. The boy carefully deposited the head-dress with his other treasures, then hastening round the corner of the barn he ran through the garden toward the large stone farmhouse owned by his father, who, on this day, had been away attending court down at Chester—an absence which, to tell the truth, was one of the main reasons for the raid on the old gobbler.

The reason for the boy's running was the fact that down the road that stretched in front of the farmhouse, he had discerned a figure on horseback coming along at a steady trot. As rather breathlessly he entered the back door the rider dismounted at the front veranda. The two met in the long hallway.

"Well, Anthony, my son," said the tall, well-set-up man as he looked down with a quizzical smile, "have you lost anything?"

"No, father," replied the boy, "not that I know of."

Isaac Wayne took something from under his arm.

"I found your school books 'tother side of the road near your Uncle Gilbert's house; I did not know whether you had dropped them."

"I left them there," said the boy frankly. "I was going to return and get them, sir."

"Too heavy to carry home, Anthony?"

"No, father, but old Jess started a rabbit

4

by the side of the road and we chased it down by the edge of the clearing. I dropped the books there.''

Mr. Wayne opened a copy book, very ragged and dog-eared. ''Will you tell me, my son, what is the meaning of all this?''

He pointed to a page covered with lines and strange markings.

''Just a plan, sir,'' the boy replied, fidgeting a little, although he was looking his father straight in the face.

''A plan of what?''

''Of a battle, father.''

''And when and where was this battle?''

''It has not been fought yet, sir. I was just making it up.''

Mr. Wayne closed the book with a smile that quite belied the seeming sternness of his next words.

''If you spent more time over your books and less in dreaming, you would make a more useful citizen, Anthony. I don't want you to grow up a know-nothing.''

''I'd like to be useful, sir.''

"Well," replied Mr. Wayne, "go out in the pasture and bring in the cows. I'll take you at your word if I have to make a farmer of you!"

"Yes, sir," said the boy, and went out of the house.

Young Anthony Wayne came quite naturally by any leaning toward military dreaming; his grandfather had been a soldier and his father had fought in the campaigns against the Indians in Western Pennsylvania and the borders of what is now Tennessee. It was in 1722 that Anthony Wayne, the grandfather of our hero, had moved from Ireland to Chester, Pennsylvania. He was a man of great independence of character, as evidenced by the fact that he had left behind him a very good country estate in County Wicklow, because he did not like the way the Irish peasantry had been treated after the defeat of the forces of King James the Second by those of King William. With this military emigrant came his wife and four sons. Three of the sons settled quite close to one another on the Pennsylvania uplands, where their father was the owner of sixteen hundred acres. The site of the old homestead is now the site of Waynesboro that has perpetuated the family name, but it is by no means the only place where it is to be found on the map. His youngest son, Isaac, possessed more of his father's character than the others, who seemed content to take up the quiet life of farmers or the sedentary occupation of a schoolmaster, which was followed by Gilbert. When the elder Anthony died he divided his estate among the three sons that survived him, and to Isaac fell the best of the farms. Isaac had married the daughter of Richard Iddings, who was also a wealthy land owner in the same county of Chester. Elizabeth Wayne was a woman of remarkable character.

Having thus introduced the younger Anthony's forebears, let us take up his life at the very interesting period when he began to develop individualities of his own. There were many of the neighbors' sons who also went to school at "Uncle Gilbert's" and many of these scholars were to be closely associated in the stirring and troublous times in the wars that were to come.

A short time, perhaps it might have been only a week or so, after his father had found his school books in the lane, Anthony, known to his comrades outside of school hours as "Shabo-na"—the Gray Fox—and the best shot with a hickory bow of all the tribes that he himself had organized, sat on a stool in the corner of the schoolhouse, looking as little like an Indian chief as any small boy could look. Instead of the crown of feathers on his head he had a conical ornament made of ordinary brown paper, on which was printed very legibly, in his Uncle Gilbert's back hand, the word, "Dunce." But if the position was ignominious it cannot be said that Anthony's demeanor was in the least humble. From under the edge of the tight-fitting paper rim he surveyed his schoolmates with a look of defiance, if not of open challenge.

He held not the slightest resentment toward his Uncle Gilbert, for he was perfectly aware that the punishment he was undergoing, if such it could be called, was well earned, but there was

a comforting thought in his mind—and in the
schoolmaster's also—that he did not care for
study; the dead languages did not appeal to him
and he had fully decided that so far as he was
concerned the longer they stayed dead the better. At figuring, when Anthony had cared to
apply himself, he was as good as any boy in
school. There were few popular histories in
those days and juvenile literature was confined
mostly to rather stupid tales that pointed ob-
vious morals or trite advice as to conduct,
habits, and spiritual training. There was
hardly a book, however, in his father's library
that dealt with anything military that Anthony
had not read from cover to cover.

There were sixteen boys in Gilbert Wayne's
school, the eldest being but fourteen. At fourteen the days of instruction practically ceased,
except for those lads whose fathers were
wealthy enough to send them to one of the col-
leges or academies in the larger towns where
the learned professions were taught. Anthony
Wayne's father was well to do and he had conceived some ambitions in regard to his son's

career, but often the boy had puzzled him, as he was now puzzling schoolmaster Gilbert, who had his own ideas of disciplining his young charges. He was one of the few schoolmasters who did not believe in the use of the rod and never had he lifted his hand in chastisement, even for breaches of behavior that deserved strenuous handling.

When the school was dismissed, this day, the boys trooped forth; one of them, Peter Iddings, a distant connection of Anthony's on his mother's side, came out last, holding something behind his back. It was the duncecap that had so lately adorned our Hero's brow. Beneath the humiliating label he had found time to print the words, "Anthony Wayne, His Hat." With some ceremony he presented it to its late wearer. No champion's gauntlet thrown in challenge ever produced a quicker result. The small boy flew at Iddings like a tiger cat. It was a battle that had long been pending between the two and it was interrupted by the appearance of the schoolmaster, who dragged the somewhat disheveled and bleeding belligerents apart and, contrary to his custom, cuffed each one soundly and leading them back into the schoolhouse, gave them a long talk on the benefits of peace in general. But, as it is with nations, so it is with individuals; it is sometimes better to have it out to a finish, for smoldering fires are more dangerous than fully extinguished ashes. Under the big red oak tree within half an hour of the schoolmaster's homily they were at it again. It was a prolonged and bitter struggle and ended in the younger boy extracting from his fallen antagonist the smothered sentence, "I've got enough." The fight established Anthony's prestige in the school. No duncecap as a bit of personal property is a disgrace to a champion fighter, and Sha-bo-na was established as one who not only must be listened to in council but respected on the battlefield.

The scholarship, however, did not improve, for it was about this time that Uncle Gilbert indited the following letter, which was handed to Mr. Wayne by no less a faithful messenger than his son:—

"I really suspect," says Gilbert, "that parental affection blinds you; and that you have mistaken your son's capacity. What he may be best qualified for, I know not; but one thing I am certain of, that he will never make a scholar. He may make a soldier; he has already distracted the brains of two-thirds of the boys, under my direction, by rehearsals of battles and sieges, etc. They exhibit more the appearance of Indians and harlequins than of students; this one, decorated with a cap of many colors; and others, habited in coats as variegated as Joseph's of old; some, laid up with broken heads, and others with black eyes. During noon, in place of the usual games and amusements, he has the boys employed in throwing up redoubts, skirmishing, etc. I must be candid with you, brother Isaac: unless Anthony pays more attention to his books, I shall be under the painful necessity of dismissing him from the school."

Isaac Wayne finished the letter without lifting his eyes to the face of the boy who, slightly flushed, was standing beside him at the old mahogany desk in his father's office. When he had finished, without comment, the father handed the letter to the boy. As the latter read, his chin trembled a little but he stood all the straighter. He knew that his father had been touched in his most vulnerable part—his pride. For a father's affections differ from those of a mother, who, no matter what her child may do, still has her heart and her arms open and her forgiveness ready before it is asked for. A father's love depends largely on his pride and his trust. It is reflective, as a mother's is instinctive.

As Anthony placed the letter back in his father's outstretched fingers he waited for what might be coming. Was it to be a punishment—a restriction of privileges? His father was a man of few words—that the boy knew well—but he could make every word a stinging blow, harder to bear than bodily chastisement. The only thing the elder Wayne said was this:

"It's in your hands, my boy."

"Then give it to me, father; let me keep it until I can hand you another one."

There was no more said.

13

CHAPTER II

THE GREAT SNOW FIGHT

IT was a very early winter—that of 1759—one long remembered for the depth of the snowfall that by the end of November covered the hills. Back at Gilbert Wayne's school were the same boys grown a little taller and heavier. One of them had changed in more than appearance. From the very first lesson of the term Anthony Wayne had shown that he had every intention of carrying out his promise to his father. So marked was this improvement that before a month had gone by Isaac Wayne had been informed that there was no fear of his son's ability to learn; the boy's ambitions had been awakened. To remain on a farm and to do the physical drudgery and to undergo the actual hardships of the pioneer farmer, was something that Anthony did not care to look forward to. He would have jumped at the opportunity to enter the Army or Navy, but very few of the sons of the Colonists at that time entered the service of the mother country, and of either Army or Navy in the proper sense the Colonies possessed none. Anthony was working toward a definite ambition, for without saying anything to anybody he had chosen his profession. There was plenty of employment for civil engineers, for the country was in a slow process of development and an engineer who had besides his technical skill a reputation for good judgment and integrity was sure of both honorable and remunerative employment. The life, also, was in the open and had in it the element of adventure. And this possibly influenced young Wayne as much as anything else in making his choice. But before he left his Uncle Gilbert he had a splendid opportunity to prove that he did, undoubtedly, possess the gift of leadership.

In the middle of the winter the only other school in Chester was disbanded on account of the sudden death of the schoolmaster. And Gilbert Wayne found the numbers of his scholars

15

exactly doubled. He was forced to take on an assistant to aid him in his teaching.

The new boys, of course, held together and brought with them the reflex of their previous companionship. Gilbert's scholars, of which young Wayne was now the leader, naturally held together also, and the result was many clashes; even the discipline of the classroom hardly prevented them at the outset from showing this feeling of antagonism. In front of the old schoolhouse the boys had built a large snow fort, and on coming to school one morning, the followers of the Gray Fox discovered that by some preconcerted arrangement the new boys held possession. They had laid in a large supply of snowballs soaked well in water, and hard as ice could freeze. Every attempt of the late comers to approach the school was with volleys of these missiles. When Anthony Wayne arrived he found his companions holding back at the edge of the little clearing. Quickly he surveyed the field, and retiring out of sight into the pine trees, laid out his plan of battle. There was a slight hill behind the

"The great snow fight."

schoolhouse and half way up a shed containing an old ox sleigh. A brilliant idea had crossed the young leader's mind. Dividing his forces, he directed Iddings to lead five boys by a circuitous route over the top of the hill and take possession of the ox wagon. It was his intention that they should come coasting down upon the rear of the snow fort, while Anthony and his little handful kept up a constant bombardment from the front, and thus claim the enemy's attention. It required some courage to face the hard frozen ice balls while replying merely with those made of the soft new-packed snow. Nevertheless, despite bruises, and in fact, much bodily discomfort, the attacking party held their ground.

Suddenly, there was a shout; down the hill came the ox wagon, steered by Iddings, and with such impetus did it strike the snow fort that it plowed through the wall, and for an instant it appeared to the astonished schoolmaster as if there would be real casualties instead of only a few bruised elbows and blackened eyes. As the ox wagon struck the rampart, Anthony led his own men forward and the battle was now one of actual conflict with hands and fists. It was interrupted by the appearance of Gilbert Wayne and his assistant, who had some work to tear the antagonists apart.

Being a man of peace, as he claimed, Gilbert Wayne was also a man of justice, and although he formally declared the action a draw, he subsequently drew Anthony to one side and gave him a private decision that undoubtedly if they had been left to fight it out his own old boys would have proved the victors.

Perhaps this little burst of confidence brought the schoolmaster and his pupil closer together than before. But it could not have been that newly awakened friendship that stirred Anthony entirely. Back in his mind was his promise to his father and a growing determination to put into his hand a letter that would entirely erase the one which his father had given him, some months before.

So well did he hold to this idea and so faithfully did he keep to his tasks that at the end of that school year he had made such progress

that Gilbert Wayne wrote the following letter
to his brother Isaac:

"Anthony has so greatly improved in his
attention to duty, his scholarship and deport-
ment, that I cannot speak of him in too high
praise. His advancement has been so rapid
during the past year that he has learned all
that I can teach him, and I recommend that he
be sent to an Academy where he may follow
any natural bent he may possess."

This letter, which was the second one of its
character that Gilbert Wayne had written, Anthony handed to his father in the little front
office of the old stone house. And then and
there he told of his ambition to take up the calling of a surveyor and civil engineer. At the
Philadelphia Academy, to which he was sent,
Anthony kept up the good record, and at the
early age of eighteen was fully competent to
take up the work of setting boundary lines,
running levels, and the use of the surveyor's
compass. Plenty of opportunity came to him
—he was always accurate and always just. His
figures and his maps might have been worked

out and made by a man of many years' experience. In 1765, when only twenty years of age, he was selected by the directors of a company that had on its lists many of the best known names in Pennsylvania, including, by the way, that of Benjamin Franklin, to go to Nova Scotia and to survey a large grant of land that had been given the company by the Crown, and upon which it was proposed to found a large settlement and farming community. He was absent quite a year and his maps and reports were spoken of as models of good workmanship, while his advice and judgment were listened to by his elders and followed out to the letter. He was now established and completely independent and, as was the way of young men in those days who were self-supporting, he looked for someone else to support also. And as soon as he came of age, in 1766, he hied himself to Philadelphia, and after a swift and victorious campaign so completely won the affections of the beautiful daughter of Bartholomew Penrose, that she capitulated after a siege of seven days and was married also in what was then almost record time. But Anthony Wayne was one of those impetuous spirits with whom decision spelt action, and as he had begun to take himself very seriously, and his whole life was filled with serious things and problems of great moment, not only to himself but to his country, it is time perhaps that we take up his life more seriously, also. No man, perhaps, has been more misjudged than the hero of Stony Point. The nickname of ''Mad Anthony'' hardly describes him, although it has been taken by many casual readers of history to describe his character.

CHAPTER III

THE PRELUDE TO GREAT DEEDS

IN the spring of 1774 Anthony Wayne had already been a farmer and surveyor for eight years. At Waynesboro, in the County of Chester, he owned and cultivated an extensive and well-ordered farm, as well as a large tannery. These were callings at which a man could become wealthy in those days, and undoubtedly young Wayne enjoyed his full share of such prosperity as his contemporaries called wealth. He was, moreover, considered the most capable surveyor in his region—the fame gained during his brief experience in Nova Scotia still endured, and had gained him a wide acquaintance; his decisions in boundary disputes among his neighbors were accepted as finalities. In addition to all these favorable conditions, Wayne was also better educated and possessed of a wider knowledge and experience of life than his immediate associates. He was endowed, moreover, with a peculiarly attractive personality that endeared him to all and valuably assisted his leadership in all public and community activities. Hence, it is not remarkable that we learn that he was widely regarded as the proper man to head any general movement among the people: he was evidently born to be a general—a fact early recognized by his schoolmaster uncle.

With all these advantages, it is to be expected, perhaps, that he might display some of the weaknesses common to humanity. We learn, accordingly, that he was somewhat vain in his manner, rather extravagant in his dress, and often given to boasting and to large assumptions. When we meet a man addicted to habits such as these we suppose, usually, that he is more capable in *talking* than in doing. With Wayne, however, as with some of the other famous men of history, it would seem that the high talk he indulged in indicated merely a creative imagination and that opportunities for action were wanting. So it was that among his neighbors his boastful speech was taken quite seriously. In fact, people seemed always to have taken him "at his own estimate of himself." Nor, as subsequent events amply proved, were they at all in error.

The coveted opportunity for action that the boy leader had so often dreamed of came at last in the exciting times just before the outbreak of the American Revolution. It was then that his ability *to do* came to be fully demonstrated. He was literally the leader among his fellows in every movement for the defense of the colonies against the hasty and ill-advised usurpations of the British Ministry, and, it is gratifying to record, he was a wise leader also. We have learned to call him "mad" Anthony Wayne, but his "madness" was not the obsession of the wanton agitator, even against aggravated abuses. Although determined in his opposition to the measures of Government to take away the autonomy of the colonies, he was to a very late date inspired with the hope that the matters in dispute might yet be settled, and the Americans reconciled with the Mother

Country. Thus, in September, 1775, as Chairman of the Chester County Committee of Safety, he wrote:

"Whereas, some persons evidently inimical to the liberty of America have industriously propagated a report that the military associators of this County, in conjunction with the military associators in general, intend to overturn the Constitution by declaring an independency . . . and as such report could not originate but among the worst of men for the worst of purposes, this Committee have thought proper to declare, and they do hereby declare, their abhorrence even of an idea so pernicious in its nature, as they ardently wish for nothing more than a happy and speedy reconciliation on constitutional principles with that State from whom they derive their origin."

Nevertheless, about a year before the date of this declaration, above quoted, Anthony Wayne had signed another which emphatically asserted the "right of every English subject to the enjoyment and disposal of his property," of which no power on earth could legally divest him, and that "the attempted invasion of that right was a grievance which should be redressed by constitutional means." From these expressions we may understand that Wayne was in hearty agreement with most of the wisest leaders of the colonists. Independence, the founding of a new nation, separate from England, was an after-thought with nearly all of them, an "evolution," as we would say today. The real grounds of contention were the attempts to abrogate the rights of self-government—placing all the colonies under the direct administration of the Crown and its ministers—and the making of laws for the colonists in which they had had no representation, in fact in regard to which they had not even been consulted. The succession of governmental blunders looking toward these ends was what made the taxation of tea, paper, etc., so odious to all Americans, especially to the people of Boston and vicinity, and was the occasion of the familiar slogan of the times, "Taxation without representation is tyranny." This latter sentence was originated, probably, in the expressions used by

THE PRELUDE TO GREAT DEEDS

John Adams, when defending John Hancock on the charge of smuggling wine in 1770, but, even with Adams and Hancock, no greater consequences were expected to their protest than the granting of the right of representation in making the laws for their own government if not for their separate government.

Such, however, was the attitude of the King and his ministers at this period that the representations of the colonists were treated with contempt. The unwise zeal of such men as Governor Edmund Andros, and others, had confirmed the opinion in England that the Americans were essentially rebellious and turbulent; and, consequently, that they were to be curbed by severe measures only. As the logical culmination to the strained relations so long existing between the Mother Country and her colonies, the incensed Bostonians plotted together and committed the depredation known as the "Boston tea party," in which a whole ship's cargo of tea was thrown overboard, because of the odious import tax. At once their city was placed under martial law. Violence now was requited with more violence, and in every case it begat its own kind; the dispute grew daily more aggravated. Even in such colonies as Pennsylvania and Virginia, where, as yet, the valued institutions of the people had not been interfered with, the conviction gained ground steadily that only an armed opposition could convince the Crown that the Americans were determined to maintain their liberties under their charters. The raising and equipping of military companies in all the colonies seemed at the time merely a measure of "preparedness" —a word that every American should know by this time and take to heart.

Among the most prominent leaders in Pennsylvania against the prevailing acts of the British Ministry was Anthony Wayne himself. In July, 1774, he was Chairman of the County Committee that adopted resolutions condemning all these acts of oppression. In January, 1775, he was a delegate to the Provincial Convention of Pennsylvania, which took measures to encourage home industries and manufactures, in opposition to the taxed imports from other countries. In the following May he originated a proposition that the "freemen" of Chester organize for military defense; later in the same year he served on the County Committees of Safety and Correspondence, and in December he was nominated for the Provincial Assembly from his County. In the meantime, also, he was busily engaged in recruiting a regiment—it was known as the Fourth Pennsylvania Battalion—and in January, 1776, attired in a resplendent uniform, he was commissioned its colonel.

With his elevation to the colonelcy of this "battalion," Wayne attained at last to the kind of position for which his instincts, abilities, and much of his previous study had amply qualified him. Even in the midst of his engrossing engagements at farming, tanning and assisting in the government and public affairs of his county and province, he had followed out his boyhood bent and had always been an eager student of military science and strategy. This is shown by his frequent references in after-life to such books as "Marshal Saxe's Campaigns," and "Cæsar's Commentaries on the Gallic War." And the idea of military essentials which he seems to have derived from his studies may be judged by the fact that he early showed marked tendencies to become a "martinet," or stickler for form and discipline. He required that each company of his command should have its own barber, and that the men should be carefully shaved, and have their hair plaited and powdered. He announced, moreover, that he would severely punish "every man who comes on parade with a long beard, slovenly dressed or dirty." In a letter to Washington, justly famous for its frankness, he says:

"I have an insuperable bias in favor of an elegant uniform and soldierly appearance, so much so that I would risk my life and reputation at the head of the same men in an attack, clothed and appointed as I could wish, merely with bayonets and a single charge of ammunition, than to take them as they appear in common with sixty rounds of cartridges. It may be a false idea, but I cannot help cherishing it."

It might seem to some readers that all such

matters are too trivial to occupy the attention of a commander of troops, whose business is, first place, "to do and to die," if, indeed, dying comes in the line of duty. But one must not forget that, just as in any mechanical device produced by human ingenuity, derangement in a small part may finally grow into a large derangement in the whole machine; so, in an organization of people, in an army or even in a deliberative assembly, all rules and regulations that promote uniformity of action and coöperation are valuable and necessary. Experience teaches us also that nothing so promotes the efficiency of a corps of soldiers as strict discipline in such small matters, as we might regard them, as those of personal appearance and behavior. We see, therefore, that Wayne showed the instincts of a real commander in his insistence on such matters, rather than the mere desire to make a fine showing on parade. The performance of his men in action throughout the war amply demonstrated the wisdom of his scheme of discipline.

CHAPTER IV

COLONEL WAYNE AT TROIS RIVIERES

IT was at the battle of Trois Rivieres, or Three Rivers, in Canada, that Colonel Wayne and his gallant command were for the first time under fire. The result of this engagement was a defeat, a defeat by no means inglorions, although, as one historian remarks, in referring to this early American reverse, they "lost almost everything belonging to them save their hair and their beards!" It was a sad blow to the members of the regiment upon whom their Colonel had expended so much care and solicitude. It was the disastrous end of an ill-conceived expedition, the attempted invasion of Canada in 1776 with the object of enlisting the sympathies and coöperation of the recently conquered French colonists in the common resistance to the British Crown. The unsuccessful assault on the stronghold of Quebec was the culmination of the failure, from which the American forces under Generals Montgomery and Arnold were compelled to make a hurried and disorderly retreat.

According to the judgment of most of the American leaders at the time, the sympathies of the French Canadians should have been easily obtained. By race and traditions alike they should have been more than willing to throw off the British yoke for the prospects of self-government. But as it happened, the policy of the Crown toward these new accessions to the British dominions had been a wise and eminently acceptable one. Probably because the main prerogative claimed by the King, direct government by the Crown through a royal governor, and without representative legislation, had already been established, it seemed possible to allow the concessions that the old French law should still hold in all administrative matters, especially land tenures, that the posts of greatest honor should be reserved, as formerly, for representatives of the French aristocracy, and, most valuable of all,

33

that the Catholic Church should be guaranteed in the possession of its vast estates. This latter provision insured the influence of the priesthood for the British, on the ground, apparently, that, since the influence and position of the Church were thus secured by law, the welfare of the people was certain to be established. Nor could the influence of even so distinguished a clergyman as the Rev. John Carroll, subsequently Catholic Archbishop of Baltimore, avail to change the attitude of his coreligionists in Canada. Undoubtedly, the Catholic priesthood and hierarchy of the province knew perfectly well that, in the event of their joining, and if the American cause were overthrown, the first movement of reprisal by the nominally Protestant State of Great Britain would be the confiscation of all Church holdings. Consequently, the mighty influence of religion was enlisted in support of the existing order, as against all the inducements offered by the American colonists and their predominantly Protestant Congress. The French Canadians assisted effectively in the defeat of the attempted invasion.

COLONEL WAYNE AT TROIS RIVIERES

Colonel Wayne's command was attached to the Pennsylvania Brigade commanded by General William Thompson, which, in addition to the Fourth Battalion, consisted of the Second Battalion, under Colonel Arthur St. Clair, and of the Sixth, under Colonel William Irvine. This force had been sent forward to assist the American army already in Canada, and started from home, undoubtedly, in high hopes of participating in a glorious and apparently certain conquest. Wayne's command, which had been variously delayed by the necessity of securing proper arms and equipment, reached a point known as Fort Sorel, midway between Montreal and Quebec, on June 5, 1776, and there joined the retreating remnant of General Montgomery's army, together with the other commands belonging to Thompson's Brigade, under the command of General John Sullivan. Immediately after their arrival, Wayne's men, together with the other Pennsylvanians, were ordered by Sullivan to attack the British force under General Burgoyne, then stationed at Trois Rivieres, some fifty miles down the river.

THE HERO OF STONY POINT

The precise advantages to be gained by making this attack are not very evident, but the Pennsylvanians responded cheerfully to the call of duty, and went forth eagerly to their baptism of fire.

The force sent to the attack on Trois Rivieres was 1,400 strong, all from Pennsylvania, except the small New Jersey Battalion, under Colonel William Maxwell. They came down the St. Lawrence River in boats, landing at a point nine miles above the town in which the British were quartered, at about two o'clock on the morning of June 9. The plan was to march forward, and to surprise Burgoyne's men about dawn, a daring plan in which, in all probability, the Americans would have been victorious. As it happened, however, they were misled on the road, came in sight of the enemy's outposts about 3 o'clock, and were compelled to make their further progress through a thick and deep swamp, in which marching was both slow and painful. After four weary hours of dark and dismal floundering, the brave Americans emerged upon an open expanse of solid ground where they were met by a large and well-formed detachment of British regulars. Although the Pennsylvanians were aided by the fact that they were proceeding through a wood, which, as Wayne himself relates, was "so deep and thick with timber and underwood that a man ten yards in front or rear would not see the men drawn up," they were also seriously disadvantaged in not being able to see other portions of their own force, and in being unable to form before reaching the open. In this difficulty Wayne's genius for generalship under conditions of actual warfare was first manifested—a man learned in the theory of strategy, a reader of books about the world's great military achievements, he proved to be a real general prepared to command! Sending for Captain Samuel Hay, he gave the brief order:

"Take you, sir, your company of riflemen, and a detachment of the light infantry of the Fourth Battalion, and advance carefully through the thicket, keeping the enemy under fire."

Having created this diversion, which, as he

stated later, was intended merely to "amuse" the enemy, he succeeded in forming the remainder of his men in good order, prepared to advance. The British, receiving the fire of Hay's men, moved forward in their direction, which was precisely the result anticipated by Wayne himself. He then moved his own men to meet the oncoming enemy, and issued his command to Hay to separate his force into two companies, one on either wing of the American line, and attempt a double flank movement, exposing the British to fire from three directions. This move was highly successful, as far as it was effective, for the British line was broken, and the men fled in disorder to their own camp. The Americans followed them up to the breastworks of their fortifications, in the face of a galling fire from musketry, field pieces and howitzers. All of the colonial forces now rushed on to follow up their advantage, including those under the command of Colonel William Maxwell, who had wandered far to the left of the other American forces in a dense thicket in the midst of the swamp. The showing made by all, who advanced with a bravery notable in men under fire for the first time, served well to impress the enemy, and to persuade them to remain within their own earthworks.

Finally, however, the combined fire of the naval vessels on the river and land forces of the British became too intense, and left no alternative but retreat. At the close of the action in the open, Wayne was left on the field with only twenty men and five officers, imperturbably directing the retreat, and retiring only when all were safely in the cover of the swamp. Even after he also had retired, he remained behind the main body of his troops to direct an incessant small fire, intended to keep the enemy within their own lines, and to cover the retreat. After about one hour he withdrew also, following a road to the point at which the party had entered the swamp in the morning, collecting in the course of the march about 700 stragglers, whom he quickly formed into order, continuing the march without further difficulty than that which comes from lack of all provisions.

About nine miles from the scene of battle a detachment of the enemy, about 1,500 strong, waylaid the Americans, and attempted to cut them off, but, separated as they were from their ships and great guns, they were able to do little dámage. Three days later, a weary band of 1,100 men, who had suffered from all sorts of hardships, including hunger and lack of sleep, reached the American camp at Fort Sorel. They had lost 300 of their number, including General Thompson and Colonel Irvine, who were taken prisoners, and Colonel St. Clair, who wandered into camp alone several hours later.

The net result of the gallant attack on Trois Rivieres was to discourage the British forces from following the Americans further, thus, as Wayne records, availing to save the army in Canada. Nor did he hesitate to claim such credit as belonged of right to his able efforts; remarking in a letter written to Dr. Franklin, "I believe that it will be universally allowed that Col. Allen and myself have saved the army." Nor was this service either needless or ill-timed. In the words of General James Wilkinson, who had been dispatched by Arnold to solicit aid in the retreat of his own forces, every house and hut on the route was "crowded with straggling men without officers, and officers without men." All were suffering from privations, and many were sick and wounded. Finally, as Wilkinson records, he met with Lieutenant-Colonel William Allen—he who seceded from the Americans after the Declaration of Independence—to whom he communicated his orders for a detachment. "Wilkinson," said Allen, "this army is conquered by its fears, and I doubt whether you can draw any assistance from it; but Colonel Wayne is in the rear, and if anyone can do it he is the man."

Wilkinson's meeting with Wayne was a memorable scene. "I met that gallant officer," he writes, "as much at his ease as if he was marching on a parade of exercise." No trace of fear or excitement was to be seen in the face or carriage of this hero, who had shown the courage of a seasoned warrior in his first experience of real fighting. He was "to the manner born," apparently, just as if there were truth in the old teaching that we are reborn into the world after death, and he had already, as he had dreamed of a former life, led his legions to victory and glory on a hundred fields of battle. On hearing Wilkinson's demand for men to assist Arnold in his extremity, Wayne acted promptly. Stationing a guard at the bridge he himself had just crossed, he gave orders to stop every man who seemed alert and capable of further immediate service, and quickly recruited a detachment sufficient for all needs. "Then," says Wilkinson, "the very men who only the day before were retreating in confusion before a division of the enemy now marched with alacrity against his main body."

Fortunately, in spite of his fears, Arnold had, meantime, succeeded in making good his escape from the trap into which the British commander had sought to draw him. Wayne missed, therefore, another immediate opportunity to achieve distinction under fire, and was obliged to return to rejoin General Sullivan at Fort Sorel. On the way back an event occurred that served to show the character of the man in a new light. When about two miles from the American camp, the detachment under Wayne's command was sighted by Sullivan's men, as it slowly made its way along the opposite bank of the Sorel River, and was mistaken for a hostile force. Wayne himself, in full sight of the American camp, viewed their hurried preparations for an attack with both amusement and surprise. He is reported to have remarked briefly:

"They should have been better prepared for an attack. Then, had we been friends or foes, our welcome would have been equally as warm."

In the retreat of the army from Canada, Colonel Wayne commanded the Pennsylvania regiments as the ranking officer—General Thompson and Colonel Irvine having been made prisoners, and Colonel St. Clair having been seriously wounded. Wayne himself had not escaped unhurt, for he had received a gun-shot wound at Trois Rivieres—he described it to Franklin as "a slight touch in my right leg"—

but he allowed himself no rest from his duties, and by his strict discipline actually transformed the straggling and disheartened crowd of his soldiers into an orderly and compacted fighting force. It was in this period, curiously enough, that he made his famous statement previously quoted, that he "would expect his officers to enforce regulations about personal cleanliness and neatness of attire," adding that he considered it their duty "to see that their men always appear washed, shaved, their hair plaited and powdered, and their arms in good order." Yet this was the man to whom much of the credit is due for leading the American forces safely out of the clutches of Burgoyne to the safe haven of Fort Ticonderoga.

CHAPTER V

ANTHONY WAYNE ASKS FOR ACTION

THE return of the American army from Canada found Anthony Wayne already famous as a capable commander and resourceful strategist. As we have already learned, the battle of Trios Rivieres had left him the ranking officer of the Pennsylvania troops, with the duty of leading them to a safe retreat at Fort Ticonderoga. The enemy's forces followed the little army—not closely, but at a safe distance. Instead of attempting a general engagement, which might have resulted injuriously to the Americans, they contented themselves with occasional skirmishes. But now followed the battle of Lake Champlain, in which Arnold's fleet was destroyed. The British, however, were content merely to threaten an attack on Ticonderoga, and then withdrew until the following season. In these days of titanic modern warfare, involving the engagement of hundreds of thousands of men, it seems a small matter indeed, the maneuvering or counter-maneuvering of a few regiments on either side. But war was a different game in those days, and important issues hung upon the outcome of a single small engagement. Both sides were uncertain, also, as to the real effective strength of their antagonists, and were naturally unwilling to risk actions that might result in disastrous defeat. The confidence of the Americans, however, is well expressed by Colonel Wayne himself, when he wrote to his wife under date January 3, 1777, "The British Rebels may be successful for a time; they may take and destroy our towns near the water and distress us much, but they never can, they never will, subjugate the free-born sons of America. Our growing country can meet with considerable losses and survive them; but one defeat for our more than savage enemies ruins them forever."

For nearly a year Wayne was stationed at Ticonderoga, then, according to general opinion, the second most important post in the whole of the colonial territory. On November 18, 1776, he was appointed by General Schuyler commandant of the fort and its dependencies, and so continued until the following April twelfth. The responsibilities of his new command, having to do with the strengthening of the extensive fortifications, and the discipline of a force of men varying between 2,500 and 7,000, who were frequently discontented with their conditions and occasionally were mutinous, fully occupied his attention. He was restive, however, at the continued lack of opportunity for real fighting and apparently exerted every means at his disposal to obtain a transference, if possible to Washington's army, which was during this same period passing through exciting adventures. The place also evidently sorely depressed his spirits, as may be judged from a remark in one of his letters:

"It [the country about Ticonderoga] appears to be the last part of the world that God made, and I have some ground to believe it was finished in the dark. That it was never intended that man should live in it is clear, for the people who attempted to make any stay have for the most part perished by pestilence or the sword. . . . The soldiers make tent pins of the shin and thigh bones of Abercrombie's men."

With all his earnest longing after more action, and his constant solicitation that he be transferred, it is gratifying to record that he wasted no time—that he seemed inspired with the ambition to discharge the duties of even an unacceptable post with the utmost care and attention. The men were frequently short on rations, were ill-equipped, were suffering constantly from the inroads of epidemic disease, and the commander exerted himself to the utmost to supply their needs—now writing long and insistent letters to his superiors, both in army and government positions, now sending requisitions to the neighboring colonies of Massachusetts and Connecticut for both men and supplies. As the result, undoubtedly, of his rigid discipline, the Pennsylvania troops won great distinction, although, in the words of Colonel Francis Johnston, the "Pennsylvanians were originally designed for soldiers," possessing a degree of "vigilance, assiduity and resignation to bad usage, fatigue and the strictest discipline."

The grand qualities of the Pennsylvania troops, be they original or from consistent discipline, found eminent illustration during the fighting following the defeat of the American fleet on Lake Champlain. The news of this disaster reached the camp at Lake George where several hundred Pennsylvanians were confined in the hospital, "emaciated with disease and sickness of the most malignant kind." But, even while many of the troops were eagerly hoping for the day of their discharge—others speaking and behaving mutinously, because compelled to remain after the expiration of their term of service, until reënforcements should arrive—the invalids and "incapacitated" rose to a man, it is related, and "fixed on their military accouterments." Then, entirely without orders or compulsion, they marched to the scene of conflict, determined to conquer or die with their countrymen. "As two privates of the First Battalion commanded by Colonel De Haas passed through our encampment,'' writes Colonel Johnston, ''they were asked if no more of the Pennsylvanians were coming, to which they answered with indignation, 'Yes, confound you, every sick man amongst us that could possibly crawl; but we led the van from our rank.' '' Some of these same men had even received their discharges, and had been kept at the hospital merely because, in the judgment of their officers and advisors, they were incapable of making the journey home. Yet these men, as Johnston relates, came ''swearing by everything sacred that they would have ample revenge!''

From his meager defensive force of not ''more than 6,000 effective men, of which something less than one-half, i. e., about 2,600, will bear the brunt of the day, the remainder being on Mount Independence on the opposite side of the Lake,'' Wayne speaks proudly in one of his letters of his own Pennsylvania contingent. ''I thank my God,'' he remarks, ''we are left partly alone. I have yet 1,500 hardy veterans from Pennsylvania; would to Heaven I could for a day lead them to the assistance of poor Washington. I would risk my soul that they would sell their lives, or liberties, at too dear a rate for Britons to make purchases." In another letter to General Schuyler he speaks of the approaching discharge of a part of this force, not without the same pride as of old, and with perfect confidence in their consistent intention to serve the cause of independence to the end of the war. "I have," he writes, "ordered one regiment of the Pennsylvania to march tomorrow [January 23, 1777]. The others will follow as soon as possible with orders to proceed in good order to Philadelphia. I have lately received letters from General St. Clair and other gentlemen in General Washington's camp which made me think it advisable to keep these regiments embodied until they are dismissed by the board of war. Their time expired the 5th of this instant: they will be settled with in Philadelphia agreeable to promise, when I have reason to expect the greatest part will reëngage."

Speaking of these same troops some time previous, Wayne remarked: " 'Liberty to come down for one month when relieved' carries with it an idea of being immediately sent back to a place [Ticonderoga] which they imagine is very unhealthy. They say, 'March us off this ground and then we will cheerfully reëngage.' Added to this, their anxiety about their friends in the Jerseys and Pennsylvania makes them impatient to be led to the assistance of their distressed home country. They likewise see the eastern people running away in the clouds of the night, some before and all soon as their times expire. Colonel Whitcomb's regiment, all the sailors and mariners, the whole of the artificers, and all the corps of artillery, except Captain Roman's company, which consists of but twelve men, officers included, are gone off the ground."

Wayne, as it seems, was incapable of understanding the motives behind such doings. Home and family were as dear to him as to any of those who, as he complains, deserted, or made a precipitous departure. But, with him, the sentiment of patriotism and the soldier's honor were altogether too high and valuable for any kind of compromise. To deserters he frequently applied the then highly opprobrious term "caitiff," which we also might consider insulting, had we not quite forgotten its use and meaning. His firm and decisive treatment of mutinous and insubordinate soldiers is exampled in the following account embodied in one of his letters:

"Yesterday morning [February 11, 1777], at gun fire, I was informed that Captain Nelson's rifle company—who used to do duty in my regiment—were under arms with their packs slung ready to march, and determined to force their way through all opposition. On my arrival at their encampment I found them drawn up in order and beginning their march. On asking the cause of such conduct, they began in a tumultuous manner to inform me that the time of their enlistment was expired last month, and that they looked upon themselves as at liberty to go home. I ordered them to halt—that I could not answer them all at once. I directed their leader to step out and speak for them. A sergeant advanced. I presented a pistol to his breast. He fell on his knees to beg his life. I then ordered the whole to ground their arms, which was immediately complied with. I then addressed them, when they with one voice agreed to remain until the 20th instant and return to their duty. This was scarce over when a certain Jonah Holida of Captain Coe's company in Colonel Robinson's regiment endeavored to excite them to mutiny again. . . . I thought proper to chastise him for his insolence on the spot before the men, and then sent him to answer for his crime to the main guard.

"The colonel waited on me and very innocently informed me that he had a complaint lodged against me, that he was very sorry for it, but was obliged to take notice of it, and then delivered the within paper. On inquiring I found it was wrote by Captain Coe. I had him brought before me. He acknowledged the writing, and also that he knew the cause for which the soldier was struck and confined, but was of the opinion that every soldier had a right to deliver his sentiments on every occasion without being punished, upon which I orderd him in arrest as an abettor of the mutiny. I wait for your orders to send them down to Albany, where you will take such further measures as you may deem necessary."

There was probably considerable reason for the dissatisfaction expressed by both Wayne and his men, who were practically marooned in a lonely and unhealthful spot, with no chance of real fighting, except with hunger, discomfort, privation and disease, and compelled to constantly urge the authorities to supply the merest necessities of life—food, clothing, ammunition and medicines. All such conditions are confidently ascribed by historians to the familiar evils, politics and incompetence in high offices. So strong, indeed, was the sentiment that "politics" even then ruled the administration of government, that, strange as it may seem at the present day, even the adoption of the Declaration of Independence was viewed without enthusiasm in many quarters, as a mere "party triumph."

On February 21, 1777, Colonel Wayne was advanced to the rank of brigadier general, and,

in spite if his tireless loyalty and efficient service to the cause of freedom, was advanced to
no higher rank during the whole period of the
war. It was not, in fact, until October, 1783,
that he was advanced by Congress to the major-
generalship, and then only by brevet. Just as
he had discharged a brigadier's duties at Ticonderoga, with only the rank and pay of a
colonel, so during the remainder of his service,
to nearly the end of the war, he did the work of
a major-general on the pay and with the rank
of a brigadier. We might strongly suspect that
"politics" had had an influence in shaping
public policy in regard to him. Yet he never
complained on this score. He was anxious only
to get more action, to lead his troops to victory
against a cruel and revengeful enemy; and with
this end attained at last, he seems to have been
actually content. In a letter to General Schuyler early in 1777 he refers to the reverses in
New Jersey and Pennsylvania, and adds that
the "alarming situation . . . causes us most
ardently to wish for an opportunity of meeting
those sons of war and rapine, face to face and

man to man." When some of his troops began to be impatient at the delay in securing their discharges, he wrote, "I want to go also. It would be in my power to do more with them in case of necessity than perhaps any other officer: I know these worthy fellows well, and they know me. I am confident they would not desert me in time of danger. If you think it would be for the benefit of the service, I should be glad to be immediately relieved in command with orders to march with the last of the southern troops."

CHAPTER VI

THE CAMPAIGN OF '77

THE day of Anthony Wayne's deliverance came at last. On April 12, 1777, he was directed by Washington to report for duty with the main body of the American army, then located at Morristown, New Jersey. He was succeeded in the command of Ticonderoga by General Arthur St. Clair, and on his arrival at Washington's camp was assigned to the command of a division of eight regiments of the newly organized Pennsylvania Line. It consisted of about 1,700 men, many of whom had been members of the original troops from Pennsylvania, and had reënlisted. He had, therefore, as nearly as possible, the realization of his long-expressed desire to command his Pennsylvania veterans in real warfare. Washington's total command at this time consisted of only five divisions, or forty-three regiments, representing a total of about 7,300 men. So Wayne was given command of about one-fourth of the effective force in men, a distinct tribute to his reputation as a capable commander.

As a matter of fact, the assignment of Wayne to this command, composed in part of seasoned troops, was no accident, nor yet even a compliment to his character and abilities. He was deliberately chosen as the best available officer to handle effective forces in an army subjected to unusual and trying conditions. A large part of Washington's command at this time was composed of fresh recruits, whose training necessarily occupied much of the time and attention of his officers. Until these men, who had been sent from several states south of the Hudson, to take the places of those whose times of enlistment had expired, it was manifestly impossible to give battle to the enemy in open field. Washington retired, therefore, to the high lands around Morristown, carefully entrenching and fortifying his positions, and maintained a "Fabian policy" of awaiting the enemy's movements until his raw recruits had been "whipped into shape." By his masterly movements in the battles of Trenton and Princeton he had compelled the enemy to retreat, and now he held the position of advantage, threatening to cut off Howe's forces in any attempt to advance on Philadelphia; also serving to protect the entrance to the country west of the Hudson River, including the way to West Point, Albany and the hill country to the south. Howe was thus subjected to the constant danger of a flank attack in any movement he might have attempted, either to attack Philadelphia, or to form a junction with General Burgoyne.

Although Washington was in a state of constant anxiety lest his position should be assaulted by a large and well-trained force of the enemy, being afraid that the comparatively unprepared condition of his own troops should be known to them, it is interesting to learn that Howe and his men were by no means as confident, nor as well informed, as might have been suspected. A small detachment under General James Grant had, to be sure, been advanced as far as Brunswick, with the apparent object in view of attempting to cut off the expected advance of General Sullivan, then at Princeton. But, instead of making any demonstration against the Americans, he carefully fortified his camp, and waited. As one historian has remarked, General Wayne seems to have "entertained a most sovereign contempt for the enemy," commenting on the fact that "they dared not face us without the cover of an entrenchment." In a letter to Sharp Delany in June, 1777, he writes:

"The enemy are all at work in fortifying their camp. We have fairly turned the tables on them, for whilst we are usefully employed in maneuvering they are at hard labor. Our people are daily gaining health, spirits and discipline—the spade and the pickaxe are throwed aside for the British rebels to take up. They, notwithstanding, affect to hold us cheap, and threaten to beat up our quarters, if we don't beat up theirs first, which is in contemplation; but of this in time."

In the repulse of the British detachment at Brunswick and its retreat to Amboy, General

Wayne played a conspicuous part. Washington had determined to dislodge them, and dispatched the Pennsylvania troops under Wayne to attack them. The result was so successful that the British withdrew hurriedly from their fortified camp "with circumstances of shame and disgrace," as Wayne expresses it. An amusing account of this affair is found in one of Wayne's letters. He writes:

"We offered General Grant battle six times the other day. He as often formed, but always on our approach his people broke and ran, after firing a few volleys, which we never returned, being determined to let them feel the force of our fire, and to give them the bayonet under cover of the smoke. This Howe, who was to march through America at the head of 5,000 men, had his coat much dirtied, his horse's head taken off, and himself badly bruised for having the presumption at the head of 700 British troops to face 500 Pennsylvanians."

The "deadlock" could not endure much longer, however. So able a general as Howe must inevitably find some means of circumventing the plans of his opponent and gaining his ends, without endangering his own safety in a flank attack, such as he must have suspected Washington was planning to deliver to a force advancing in any direction. Accordingly, Howe solved the difficulty by determining to transport by sea a force sufficient to attack Philadelphia, and toward the end of July, 1777, withdrew his troops from New Jersey, and embarked them at Staten Island. About the same time that the news of this movement was received at the American camp, the unbelievable disaster of the capture of Fort Ticonderoga was also communicated to them. This fort, so carefully fortified by Wayne, at the expense of time, labor and human lives—for many men contracted disease in the prosecution of the work—had one absurdly weak point. The fortifications were commanded by the heights of Mount Defiance to the rear, a fact pointed out by both Wayne and Trumbull some months before, but without success in persuading the authorities to provide for the occupation of this position. The British, however, were not slow to seize the advantage so invitingly afforded them, and when their guns and men were perceived there, General St. Clair immediately capitulated, without firing a shot, or attempting any resistance. They were well prepared for a long siege, also to repel assaults on their works, but not to suffer from the galling fire of a battery mounted on the heights to their rear.

Astounding as the new complication of affairs must have seemed, Washington was equal to the emergency. He was convinced that he had nothing to fear from the forces of Burgoyne in the north. Consequently his attention was devoted to providing to prevent the capture of Philadelphia. With this object in view, he issued these orders to General Wayne:

"The fleet having gone out of the Hook, and as Delaware appears to be its most probable destination, I desire that you will leave your brigade under the next in command, and proceed to Chester County, in Pennsylvania, where your presence will be necessary to arrange the militia who are to rendezvous there."

In obedience to this order, Wayne at once

returned to his home county, and plunged into the midst of the heavy work of organizing the militia. So quickly was the final work accomplished that on August 23, about one month after Howe's departure from New York, the forces were sent to the front, marching through Philadelphia on the way to Wilmington. Even though so near to his home at this time, Wayne could not even visit his family, and saw them but once, apparently, during the entire period. This may be judged from a letter written to his wife on August 26:

"I am peremptorily forbid by His Excellency to leave the army. My case is hard. I am obliged to do the work of three general officers. But if it was not the case, as a general officer, I could not obtain a leave of absence. I must, therefore, in the most pressing manner, request you to meet me tomorrow evening at Naaman's Creek. Pray bring Mr. Robinson, with my little son and daughter."

About three days after the writing of this letter to his wife, Wayne had arrived with his division, which had followed him from Washington's camp, at the American position near Wilmington. There preparations were immediately begun to meet the enemy's forces, which were reported advancing from the landing place on Chesapeake Bay. The eastern shore of the Brandywine River was selected as the most advantageous position to meet the expected attack, or, at least, to prevent the British forces from crossing the river, as was expected, at a place known as Chad's Ford. Wayne evidently examined the ground thoroughly, and made a strong recommendation to Washington, in a letter dated September 2, that a strong detachment of the American army be detailed to make a flank attack on the British as they were attempting to advance. This opinion he fortified by copious references to the strategies of Cæsar and other great commanders of the past, who by sudden flank movements had succeeded in routing and demoralizing an already all-but-victorious enemy. The plan did not seem to have appealed to Washington's judgment, since he directed the plan of battle on an entirely different theory. The American forces drew up near Chad's Ford, and attempted to prevent the enemy from reaching it, but, in spite of exceptional bravery and a most determined defense, were finally compelled to retreat.

In this fight, as was quite to his liking, undoubtedly, Wayne bore the brunt of the severest fighting, his force being directly fronted by the seven thousand Hessians under Baron Wilhelm von Knypenhausen, who vainly attempted until sunset to pass by and gain the ford. Then, however, he was compelled to retire, even though in good order, because of the fact that his supports had been driven from the field, when the two divisions under Generals Sullivan and Greene, forming the right wing of the American line, had been turned back by the fierceness of Cornwallis' assaults. Wayne was then compelled to retire, Knypenhausen being in front and Cornwallis in the rear.

Undoubtedly, had it not been for the tenacity and courage of the British regulars, the outcome would have been different, perhaps even a complete American victory. Despite the fear and hatred of them felt by their contemporary enemies, these "Hessians" of Knypenhausen's were a poor lot of people. They were not the trained German soldiers of the present day, but miserable creatures, recruited, for the most part, from workhouses and by press gangs, according to the custom of the Eighteenth Century in all European countries. They were frequently compelled to fight for the cause in which they had no earthly interest, by threats and compulsion, and large numbers of them seized any available opportunities to desert. Wayne's men deserved high credit, undoubtedly, for successfully withstanding for so long a time the fierce assaults of an overwhelmingly superior force, but, apart from the fact that, in those days, at least, it would have taken a long time to kill and disable a force of seven thousand men, or even to drive them off, they might easily have withstood them indefinitely. From the standpoint of our knowledge of operations in recent wars, with the terrible engines of destruction now in use, it seems difficult, indeed, to understand the conditions of military fighting at the period of the Revolution. Usually, in musketry fighting, at least, the two opposing forces would line up opposite one another and continue firing until an opportunity appeared to adopt other tactics. That such affrays were not more bloody than they were can be ascribed only to the inefficiency at long range of the muskets of the period, combined with general poor marksmanship. Thus, as records show, one regiment engaged at Brandywine—the Thirteenth Pennsylvania, commanded by Colonel Walter Stewart—lost but sixteen men in this battle and in the later affray at Germantown. The nature of the fighting done by this corps may be judged from the following account left by one of its lieutenants, James MacMichael:

"We attacked the enemy at 5:30 P. M., and we were first obliged to retreat a few yards, and formed in an open field, when we fought without giving way on either side until dark. Our ammunition almost expended, firing ceased on both sides, when we received orders to proceed to Chester. This day for a severe and excessive engagement exceeded all I ever saw. Our regiment fought at one stand about an hour under an incessant fire, and yet the loss was less than at Long Island, neither were we so near to each other as at Princeton, our common distance being fifty yards."

Undoubtedly, the greatest danger to such a force would have been its envelopment by the enemy, with close-quarters fighting, in which bayonets would be used and the sheer physical force of a massed weight of men would have been the greatest factor on either side. It was to avoid this very disaster—the speedy crushing out of its life by the superior numbers of the enemy on both sides—that the right wing retired before Cornwallis, and later, also, the center, under Wayne himself, before the hordes of Knypenhausen. Wayne's retreat did cover the rear of Sullivan and Greene, discouraging any attempt to follow by the British regulars. Thus the American forces were able to retire in good order, even retrieving several pieces of artillery which had been deserted on the field. A spirited account of the rescue of the guns is left for us by one of the American officers (Colonel William Chambers), who writes:

"The general sent orders for our artillery to retreat, and ordered me to cover it with a part of my regiment. It was done, but, to my surprise, the artillerymen had run and left the howitzer behind. The two pieces went up the road protected by about sixty of my men, who had very warm work, but brought them safe. I then ordered another party to fly to the howitzer and bring it off. Captain Buchanan, Lieutenant Simpson, and Lieutenant Douglass went immediately to the gun, and the men following their example, I covered them with the few I had remaining [Wayne aimed and fired one of the field pieces himself]; but before this could be done the main body of the foe came within thirty yards and kept up the most terrible fire ever heard in America, though with very little loss on our side. I brought all the brigade artillery safely off, and I hope to see them again fired at the scoundrels. Yet we retreated to the next height in good order in the midst of a very heavy fire of cannon and small-arms. Not thirty yards distant we formed to receive them, but they did not choose to follow."

CHAPTER VII

THE American forces retired in good order, and that same night encamped at Chester, eleven miles from the field of battle. On the following day they marched sixteen miles to Schuylkill Falls, with the intention of forming a junction with Washington's army and barring the road to Philadelphia. In the operations preceding the occupation of that city by the British there seem to have been a long series of unfortunate circumstances. Letters containing important commands were lost, or captured by the enemy, and Wayne, Greene, and other commanders were left to follow former orders, to the disarrangement of Washington's astutely conceived plans to oppose the advance. But for such unfortunate occurrences, coupled with the information given to the enemy by Tory spies, it is more than probable that the British could, even then, have been held off. This opinion seems to have been shared by contemporary writers, among them Wayne himself, who records in one of his numerous letters of the action near Pawling Mill that, but for several unfortunate causes of confusion, they might have achieved a "victory that in all human probability would have put an end to the American war."

Such explanations of conditions are necessary, in order to explain the apparent dereliction of General Wayne, which led to his trial by court-martial on serious charges specifying neglect of duty. These charges grew out of a most unfortunate affair: the attempted surprise of his camp, known to history as the "Paoli Massacre." Wayne, according to orders from General Washington, had encamped his division at a point on the old Lancaster road, midway between the Paoli and Warren taverns, in order to be in position to attack the British rear guard on the following morning, it being his intention to capture its baggage train. He had advanced with the

73

greatest secrecy, as was necessary in any such undertaking, but missed the golden opportunity to lead a brilliant and, perhaps, successful action through the treachery of some Tory spies, who betrayed the location of his encampment. Consequently, the British rear guard commander determined in his turn upon a surprise attack, which was partially successful, although, as Wayne claims, and his superiors were convinced on his representation, he had been previously informed of the intended attack and posted his guards with his usual care. The enemy came on in such numbers, however, that they were able to "rush" the guards, and were upon the camp before the formation of troops had been completed. Indeed, as one historian remarks, they had "a force so large that two of the British regiments of which it was composed were not engaged in the horrible work in which the rest were so conspicuous, their services not being required." Wayne's report of the affair is as follows:

"About 11 o'clock last evening (September 20, 1777) we were alarmed by a firing from one of our out guards. The division was immediately formed, which was no sooner done than a firing began on our right flank. I thought proper to order the division to file off by the left, except the infantry and two or three regiments nearest to where the attack began, in order to favor our retreat. By this time the enemy and we were not more than ten yards distant. A well-directed fire mutually took place, followed by a charge of bayonet. Numbers fell on each side. We then drew off a little distance, and formed a front to oppose to theirs. They did not think prudent to push matters further. Part of the division are a little scattered, but are collecting fast. We have saved all our artillery, ammunition and stores, except one or two wagons belonging to the commissary's department.''

With the curious reluctance, so often noted by contemporary writers, the British troops neglected to follow up the advantage already gained, although, with their superior force, they might have inflicted even further damage upon the American lines. As at Brandywine, and at other engagements still to be recorded, the probabilities are that a determined advance upon the retreating foe would have transformed defeat into a rout, and made future progress far easier. We must not forget, however, that any such pushing on after an advantage meant precisely one thing, "cold steel"—and man-to-man fighting is distinctly repugnant to the modern soldier. It is one of the results following the use of firearms as the principal element in battle. Nothing could better illustrate this contention than the fact that this affair has been always known as a "massacre." Sixty-one Americans were killed, mostly by the bayonet, and the "atrocity" of the thing long oppressed patriotic minds and imaginations. The same popular "horror" was also visited, in part, upon Wayne himself, who was roundly blamed, first, for pitching his camp so near to the enemy, and second, for providing insufficient guards to prevent the disorder following an attack. A court of inquiry found against him on both these charges, and he immediately demanded a court martial, by which he was thoroughly acquitted. His defense was that his camp was at least two miles from that of the enemy, and that it could not have been otherwise located, in obedience to Washington's commands, and in view of the fact that he was expecting to make a junction with the force under General William Smallwood. He was also vindicated on the matter of properly placed guards. The entire affair consisted in the confusion due to loss of letters from Washington, directing changes of plans outlined in previous orders. These letters probably fell into the hands of the enemy, and enabled them to circumvent all movements made by Wayne.

Thus, three times within a week Washington had changed his orders, on account of the changing conditions in the situation. On September 15 Wayne had arrived at the White Horse Tavern on the Lancaster Road, with the intention of carrying out his orders to make a flank movement against the British army as it attempted to ford the river. Here a small skirmish occurred on the following day. On the seventeenth the orders were again changed, so that, as already stated, Wayne should be able to take a position from which he could attack the enemy's rear while the main army under Washington should resist its passage of the fords. Finally, both orders were rescinded, and Wayne was ordered to join Washington at Potts' Grove. Owing, perhaps, in part to the confusion following the non-delivery of these letters of command, the original plans miscarried, and Howe forced his way to Philadelphia. Before attempting to occupy the city, however, the British commander dispatched large detachments of his troops to reduce the American fortifications at Billingsport, Mud Island and Red Bank on the Delaware River, in order to gain free access for the fleet in bringing up supplies. Thus, with an apparent lack of good judgment, he left himself in a weakened condition in his camp within a few miles of the city. Washington, acting on his own opinion, and against the strongly urged judgments of ten out of his thirteen general officers—only Generals Wayne, Smallwood and Scott favored it—determined to attack the British before their detached columns could return to camp, and without waiting for the reënforcements expected from the north.

In the arrangement of the line of battle the right wing was assigned to the command of General Sullivan, to whose division that of Wayne was also added. The left wing was under the command of General Greene, but, most unfortunately, did not succeed in reaching the field in time to join in the battle. Several other corps failed to make a good showing in the fight, with the result that, as seems to have been his fate on numerous occasions, Wayne's men bore the brunt of nearly the hardest fighting of the day. Indeed, had all the troops been of the same mettle, and under as good discipline as those under Wayne, it is not improbable that the British army would have been utterly crushed.

The most interesting part of the whole affair, for the present, at least, is the experience of Wayne and his men. Here, again, as in many other instances, he has left us a clear account of the day's doings in his familiar and graphic style. In a letter to his wife, written two days after the fight, he writes:

"On the 4th instant at the dawn of day we attacked General Howe's army at the upper end of Germantown. The action soon became general. When we advanced on the enemy with charged bayonets, they broke at first without waiting to receive us, but soon formed again, when a heavy and well-directed fire took place on each side. The enemy again gave way, but, being supported by the grenadiers, returned to the charge. General Sullivan's division and Conway's brigade were at this time engaged to the right or west of Germantown, whilst my division had the whole right wing of the enemy's army to encounter, on the left or east of the town, two-thirds of our army being then too far to the east to afford us any assistance. However, the unparalleled bravery of the troops surmounted every difficulty, and the enemy retreated in the utmost confusion. Our people, remembering the action of the night of the 20th of September, near the Warren, pushed on with their bayonets, and took ample vengeance for that night's work. Our officers exerted themselves to save many of the poor wretches who were crying for mercy, but to little purpose; the rage and fury of the soldiers were not to be restrained for some time, at least not until great numbers of the enemy fell by our bayonets. The fog, together with the smoke occasioned by our cannon and musketry, made it almost as dark as night. Our people, mistaking one another for the enemy, frequently exchanged several shots before they discovered their error. We had now pushed the enemy near three miles, and were in possession of their whole encampment, when a large body of troops were discovered advancing on our left flank, which being taken for the enemy, we retreated. After retreating for about two miles, we found it was our own people, who were originally designed to attack the right wing of the enemy's army. The fog and this mistake prevented us from following a victory that in all human probability would have put an end to the American war. General Howe for a long time could not persuade himself that we had run from victory, but the fog clearing up he ventured to follow us with all his infantry, grenadiers and light horse, with some field pieces. I, at this time, was in the rear, and, finding Mr. Howe determined to push us hard, drew up in order of battle, and waited his approach. When he advanced near we gave him a few cannon shot with some musketry, which caused him to run with the utmost confusion. This ended the action of the day, which continued without intermission from daylight until near twelve o'clock."

Wayne's account is graphically supplemented by another from the pen of General Hunter of the British army. He writes:

"The first that General Howe knew of Washington's marching against us was by his attacking us at daybreak. General Wayne commanded the advance and fully expected to be avenged for the surprise we had given him. When the first shots were fired at our pickets, so much had we all Wayne's affair in remembrance that the battalion were out under arms in a minute. . . . Just as the battalion formed, the pickets came in and said the enemy were advancing in force. They had barely joined the battalion when we heard a loud cry, 'Have at the bloodhounds, revenge Wayne's affair!' and they immediately fired a volley. . . . We charged them twice till the battalion was so reduced by killed and wounded that the bugle was sounded to retreat; indeed, had we not retreated at the time we did we should all have been taken or killed, as two columns of the enemy had nearly got round our flank. But this was the first time we had ever retreated from the Americans, and it was with great difficulty we could get the men to obey our orders.

"The enemy were kept so long in check that two brigades had advanced to the entrance of Beggarstown, when they met our battalion retreating. By this time General Howe had come up, and seeing the battalion retreating, all broken, he got into a passion, and exclaimed, 'For shame, Light Infantry, I never saw you retreat before. Form! Form! It is only a scouting party.' However, he was quickly convinced that it was more than a scouting party as the heads of the enemy's columns soon appeared. One coming through Beggarstown with three pieces of cannon in their front immediately fired with grape at the crowd that was standing with General Howe under a large chestnut tree. I think I never saw people enjoy a discharge of grape before, but we really felt pleased to see the enemy make such an appearance, and to hear the grape rattle about the Commander-in-Chief's ears, after he had accused the battalion of having run away from a scouting party."

CHAPTER VIII

VALLEY FORGE AND THE LONG DARK DAYS

IN spite of the gallant behavior of the American troops at the Battle of Germantown, in which, as Wayne writes, they were all but victorious, or, at least, must have been, but for certain untoward happenings and ill-judged arrangements, the British army succeeded in occupying Philadelphia. The next reverse of the American cause lay in the capture of the forts on the Delaware River, which had hitherto effectually prevented the British ships from reaching the army at Philadelphia with supplies. In the first place, lack of sufficient available forces for defense had led early to the abandonment of the post at Billingsport, in order to strengthen those at Red Bank and Mud Island nearer to the city. Both these places had been effectively fortified, and were able to withstand a determined attack by a large force of "Hessian" troops on October 22, repulsing them finally with the loss of 200 men and their commander, Count Donop. With the intention of applying a more promising method of attack, Howe then planted a strong battery on Province Island, opposite to Fort Mifflin on Mud Island, and made elaborate preparations to bombard the works. Washington, although strongly urged by several of his advisors—Wayne among them—to assault and destroy these new works, declined, on the ground that his forces were insufficient, and that nothing could be done before the arrival of reënforcements from the north. In spite of this decision of the Commander, Wayne made the bold suggestion that he be allowed with his corps to attempt the capture of Howe's batteries, but this proposal also was rejected. So, with the policy of caution consistently adhered to, the result was that Howe completed his preparations without interference, and, in his own good time, proceeded to cannonade Fort Mifflin, compelling the garrison to withdraw, after a gallant defense, simply because there was no fort left to defend.

This defense Washington characterized as calculated to "reflect the highest honor upon the officers and men of the garrison."

It seems regrettable, indeed, that no attack on the British battery was attempted, and that General Wayne thus missed an opportunity to add still further to the record of his glorious deeds. That he would have given an excellent account of himself in any such attempt cannot be doubted. He might even have been successful. Fort Mifflin fell on October 15, 1777, thus closing a campaign full of brilliant deeds of bravery neutralized by one long succession of blunders and miscarriages of plans, which served to snatch victory from the very grasp of the American patriots over and over again.

The season was then so far advanced that further operations had to be delayed until the spring of 1778, and the dreary and dismal days of Valley Forge began. While, as there can be no doubt, the American cause was largely hampered by actual poverty and the difficulty of always obtaining necessary supplies at the time required, it is also humiliating to record that further obstacles were interposed by political corruption, official incompetence and an almost unbelievable tendency to subordinate public necessity to personal considerations. Thus, while Washington's army, which had been so carefully preserved from the risks of unsupported attacks on Province Island, and other points, were suffering at Valley Forge from lack of clothing, shoes, and even food, all kinds of preposterous excuses were made for the wanton delay in supplying these necessities. Particularly conspicuous for dereliction in this respect was the Clothier-General of Pennsylvania, a certain James Mease, who actually refused to supply the clothing needed for the soldiers, without a properly attested Order of Council, and even then persisted in all kinds of delays until the winter was passed and spring again opened.

Unless history entirely misrepresents this gentleman, he was a wholly incompetent blockhead, swelled with the pride of an important office, and far more solicitous to obtain personal adulation, and to persist in his own methods of doing things, than to see that the soldiers were properly cared for. He seems to have spent a large part of his time in traveling from home, and on his return to have observed a policy, which he may have considered "economical," of retaining as much cloth as possible in storage. In striking contrast to such a person stands the heroic figure of Anthony Wayne, who, unmindful, as usual, of the hardships suffered by himself, wrote constantly, and at great length, to the authorities, urging, protesting, complaining and demanding, as action on the matter of supplies was constantly delayed. From January until April he wrote these letters to anyone and everyone who could at all avail to assist him, if so disposed; to Richard Peters, Secretary of War, to Thomas Wharton, President of Pennsylvania, to the Speaker of the State Assembly, and to the nearly unapproachable Clothier-General himself. But even the best and ablest of these people seems to have been so hampered in his powers by party conflicts, incompetence in responsible positions and general "red tape," that nothing resulted from any of them save promises and excuses, the latter almost as ingenious as absurd. Thus, his appeal to the State President (or Governor) is answered by the allegation that the clothing asked for had been prepared, but that its delivery was being held up because of the "want of buttons." On another occasion the excuse is that an "immense quantity of clothing" had been ordered, and that its non-delivery was a real mystery. In order to expedite matters somewhat, Wayne ordered and purchased a quantity of cloth for uniforms, which he purposed having made up in camp, but he was informed that the merchants declined to deliver "until they know where to receive their pay," and that "the Clothier-General has peremptorily refused paying Col. Miller's orders in favor of these merchants."

Late in March, after nearly three months of hunger, cold and nakedness in camp, Wayne dispatched Colonel Stephen Bayard to Lancaster with requisitions for the sorely needed supplies. Nearly four weeks later, on April

23, this officer wrote from Lancaster, as follows:

"Mr. Mease came home yesterday, and consented at last to let me have linen for twelve-hundred shirts, provided it could be made up here. Mr. Howell, Major Werts and myself engaged it should, and for that purpose we have been in and through every family in this town, in order to get them made up, and I have the satisfaction to inform you that they are to be ready in eight days from this. As the expenses of staying here are great, I would gladly know whether I must remain, and bring them with me, or come immediately to camp. It gives me pain to relate the difficulty of getting anything from Mease. Waiting his slow motion, dancing attendance, etc., are insufferable. Had I full powers, it should be otherwise, but he prides himself upon his being confined to no particular state."

Even at this late date matters progressed with the familiar slowness. Supplies of necessities that should have been promptly dispatched to camp continued to come in in small quanti-

ties. On one occasion, Wayne relates in a
pathetic letter to Mr. Peters the whole situation
and gives a pen picture of Valley Forge: "I
hoped to be able to clothe the division under my
command, but the distresses of the other part
of the troops belonging to this state were such
as to beggar all description. Humanity obliged
me to divide what would have in part clothed six
hundred men among thirteen regiments, which
was also necessary in order to prevent mutiny."

In another letter to Mr. Peters, he writes,
after a brief absence: "On my arrival in camp
I found the division in a much worse condition
for the want of clothing and every other matter
than I had expected. I am endeavoring to
remedy the defects, and hope soon to restore
order, introduce discipline and content, all which
was much wanting and desertion prevailing fast.
I flatter myself that I have so much the esteem
and confidence of my troops that desertion will
no longer take place. I am happy to inform you
that there is not a single instance since my
return."

In another place he remarks in a way that

shows the depths of misery achieved at the camp: "I am not fond of danger, but I would most cheerfully agree to enter into action once every week in place of visiting each hut of my encampment (which is my constant practice), and where objects strike my eye and ear whose wretched condition beggars all description. The whole army is sick and crawling with vermin."

The bitter fruits of official incompetence and corruption, including the excuseless blunder of retaining such creatures as Mease in important positions, and the preposterous wranglings of opposing parties in the state councils, had doomed hundreds of brave men to the hardships mentioned. For they did not suffer from cold alone, nor even from difficulty in always securing food, as was perhaps inevitable, but from the utter lack of necessities that could readily have been supplied by a well-organized and efficient management, for the government, though sometimes pressed for money, was by no means bankrupt. As late as May 4, 1778, Wayne wrote to President Wharton:

"Enclosed is the return of the thirteen regiments belonging to the state of Pennsylvania. You will observe that they are very weak. The chief part of those returned sick at present is for want of clothing, being too naked to appear on the parade. Our officers in particular are in a most wretched condition. I can't conceive the reason why they are not supplied. I purchased cloth, etc., at York, last January sufficient to clothe a great part of them, but have not heard what has been done with it. I know it must be distressing to your excellency to hear so many repetitions of our wants, but whatever pain it may give you, I hourly experience much more from the complaints and view of worthy fellows, who are conscious of meriting some attention, and whose wretched condition can not be worse. They think any change must be for the better, and too many have risked desertion. The enclosed order has lately put some stop to it, and had we clothing I am confident that we should not have any more leave us, where we now have twenty."

In view of all the difficulties besetting him daily, it is scarcely remarkable that Wayne writes in one of his letters to Peters, in the latter part of January, as nearly a complaint as ever escaped him. "I am too much interested in the freedom and happiness of America," he says, "to withdraw from the army at this crisis. I believe I have a much greater share of care and difficulty than ought to come to the proportion of one officer. Unfortunately, there is no other general in the Pennsylvania Line belonging to this army. We derive but little assistance from the civil authority, and every let and hindrance in the power of the Clothier-General seems to be thrown in the way. So that I am almost tempted to. But I will, at all events, provide for my poor fellows before I consult my own ease and happiness."

There was never any intention in Anthony Wayne's mind of resigning. He only hoped to convey the bitterness of his feelings. But while he and other commanding officers were engaged in struggling to keep their soldiers from dying of starvation, cold and disease, Congress saw fit to still further embarrass their efforts to secure order and efficiency by the

passage of laws cutting the pay of military officers, or rather providing that they receive their
remuneration for services in the form of half
pay for seven years after the end of the war.
This may have been a necessary step—it probably was, in the almost exhausted state of
finances, but it created great opposition and
disaffection among those immediately affected,
many of whom were by no means wealthy, none
of them favorably impressed with the idea of
the buying power of the then greatly depreciated currency. Wayne, as usual, sincere patriot
that he was, took the most favorable view of the
matter, and registered no complaints whatever
on his own behalf. His remarks upon the
matter were concerned solely with the sufferings of others. In a letter to a good friend of
his, Sharp Delany, in May, 1778, he writes:

"The difficulty I experience in keeping good
officers from resigning, and causing them to
do their duty in the line, has almost determined
me to give it up, and return to my Sabine fields,
but I first wish to see the enemy sail for the
West Indies. . . . For my own part, I have a

competency, and neither look nor wish for any gratuity, other than liberty and honor; but the discontented say that seven years' half pay would not near make up for the depreciation of the money."

Only the spirit of self-sacrifice and the great devotion to a great cause kept the little army together during the dark days of the winter of '77.

CHAPTER IX

DURING the long, hard winter at Valley Forge, amid all the sufferings resulting from hardship and official neglect, such preparations as were possible for soldierly efficiency were constantly in progress. Most conspicuous, perhaps, among these was the engagement of Baron Wilhelm von Steuben, a Prussian general of high reputation, who, from generous interest in the cause of American liberty, had freely offered his services to help train the army. Although without friends or connections in this country, and wholly ignorant of the English language, he cheerfully worked at the difficult task of drilling and training the raw troops in Washington's camp in the manual of arms and the maneuvers familiar to the armies of Europe. He is credited with promoting singular efficiency in bayonet work—some have said that he introduced the bayonet to the American army, which seems to be untrue, as it was an inheritance from their British ancestry. But he is to be credited, undoubtedly, with originating much of the efficiency displayed by the troops in the succeeding campaign. Such men as Steuben, Lafayette, and our own Wayne, who continued working and fighting for an ideal, even in the face of all the discouragements heaped up by nature and by human rascality, are as bright and shining lights in the midst of otherwise cheerless prospects. Why can not the noble examples of such heroic characters oftener excite the reverence and emulation of the rest of the world? They were men, indeed!

We have learned already of Wayne's untiring efforts to secure from Congress, as well as from the Government of Pennsylvania, relief for the sufferings of his soldiers. We have read of the specious promises, pompous excuses and shifty evasions of public duty, not only on the part of the inglorious and useless Mease, but even from those who stood higher and much better in official life. But, as if all his labors had been in vain, and all his protests and petitions unheard, we read in a letter from Wayne to Sharp Delany, under date May 13, 1778, the following piteous appeal:

"For God's sake give us, if you can't give us anything else, give us clean linen that we may be enabled to rescue the poor, worthy fellows from the vermin which are devouring them. . . . Some hundreds we thought prudent to deposit some six feet under ground, who have died of a disorder produced by a want of clothing. The whole army at present are sick of the same disorder, but the Pennsylvania line seem to be the most infected. A pointed and speedy exertion of Congress or appointing another doc'r [doctor?] may yet remove the disorder, which once done I pledge my reputation we shall remove the enemy. For I would much rather risk my life and honor and the fate of America on our present force neatly and comfortably uniformed than on double their number covered with rags and crawling with vermin. But I am determined not to say another word on the subject."

REAR GUARD FIGHTING

Even Anthony Wayne had at last reached the limit of his patience with official incompetence and the criminal neglect of the brave men under him. He vowed to say no more upon the subject, and no more did he say. His soldiers went forth in rags to meet a well-disciplined and thoroughly equipped army, and, thanks almost wholly to the inspiration of their brave commander, did more than their duty.

Until nearly the middle of June the army remained in camp, availing themselves of such reliefs to their sufferings as were occasionally afforded. At the same time the able-bodied were constantly drilling and maneuvering under the direction of Steuben and other drill masters. In the meantime only an occasional light skirmish had occurred with the enemy, notably one in the middle of May, in which a strong British force from Philadelphia attempted to flank and surround a detachment of about 2,500 men, sent under Lafayette to occupy the city, upon their expected evacuation. The Americans escaped without losses, but their rear guard, backed by a troop of Oneida Indians, put the enemy to flight with some serious damage.

The long-expected evacuation of Philadelphia occurred on June 18th, when the entire British army, under the command of Sir Henry Clinton, crossed the Delaware River below Gloucester, and took its march to the eastward through New Jersey. The forces, in excellent condition, after a winter of ease and comfort in the city, consisted of about 12,000 men, and were followed by a baggage train twelve miles long. Three days later Washington, with his entire command, crossed the Delaware above Trenton, and proceeded to cautiously follow the enemy, with a view either to dispute his passage of the Raritan River, or of cutting off his baggage train. For a considerable distance he paralleled the British line of march, sometimes at a distance of only a few miles. Finally he held a council of his generals to fix upon a method of attack. As usual, the majority of these people were in favor of a "Fabian policy," as it were, or a continuation of extreme caution in any moves to attack so powerful a body. Only Wayne, supported in this case by General John

Cadwalader, and partially by Generals Greene and Lafayette, advocated an immediate and vigorous attack. Washington, as on several other occasions, rejected the advice of his other officers, and adopted that given by Wayne; determining to attempt a surprise on the enemy's rear guard, so as to harass the baggage train, and capture as much of it as possible. He accordingly asked Wayne to outline his plan in a letter to himself, and followed the advice given in all of the main details.

The plan of action adopted was that a detachment of about 5,000 men under the command of General Charles Lee and Marquis de Lafayette was ordered to hang on the enemy's rear, and attack him as soon as possible in the morning; the remainder of the army being held in reserve to support this detachment, in case of repulse. For, as Wayne confidently asserted in his letter to Washington, the "enemy dare not pursue success, lest they be drawn into some difficulty from which it would not be easy for them to extricate themselves."

The appointment of Charles Lee to lead this

attack was, if possible, nearly the greatest error that could have been committed at the time. His sole apparent qualification for the service was that he had been appointed by some order of official favoritism to the rank of a major general. But such soldierly qualities as he may have possessed were exceeded by his laggard methods and his personal animosities. The latter evil trait was well demonstrated when, on the morning of the battle of Monmouth (June 28, 1778), he ordered Wayne to proceed with a detachment of 1.200 men and attack the British left rear.

"This, Sir, is a post of conspicuous honor, worthy of so brave an officer as yourself, and I trust that you will acquit yourself worthily in the performance of the duties which it implies," was his supercilious address to Wayne.

That he may have hoped that the "honor" involved would also mean Wayne's permanent removal from all military activity, thus relieving the army for all time of "so noisy and boisterous a fellow" [as he had often characterized him], is strongly suggested by his own behavior.

Instead of remaining with the balance of his division to support Wayne's men, he almost immediately withdrew, greatly to the disgust of his own command, and to the exasperation of Washington himself, who promptly ordered him court-martialed. In his attempted defense, this "caitiff," as Wayne would probably have called him, had he been speaking to intimates, sought to accuse Wayne of disobedience to orders, and to besmirch the characters of several other prominent officers. The result was that he was promptly challenged to duels by Wayne, by Colonel John Laurens, and by the brave and soldierly Steuben himself. But, enough of Lee; his record is part of history.

Wayne went forward with joy [to his death, as Lee probably supposed], and promptly engaged the rear of the enemy. His attack was met by a body of American tories, known as Simcoe's Rangers, who made a furious charge upon the Pennsylvania regiment commanded by Colonel Richard Butler, a devoted friend of Wayne's, and his constant companion in arms until the end of the war. Butler's men fired a tremendous volley of musketry, which threw their assailants into disorderly retreat, but the advantage could not be followed up, because of the lack of cavalry. At this juncture the main body of the British rear began to advance, a force estimated at about 2,000 men, which was rapidly increased by new detachments from the front. This was the condition in which Lee was to have supported Wayne, in order to prevent the annihilation of his command. But Lee failed him; he was already withdrawing his men to a safe distance. Nothing remained for Wayne, therefore, but to follow him ignominiously. At the old Tennent Church, on the road to Freehold, Lee met Washington, who, as reported, was "angry beyond restraint." That Lee's career was not terminated on the spot was due, undoubtedly, to the fact that Washington was just and humane, even in "anger unrestrained." However, it is reported that the usually calm Washington used stormy language.

As events proved, Lee's stupid or intended blunder endangered not only Wayne and his men, but also General Washington himself, and narrowly escaped exposing the entire army to an assault in force by the enemy that might have led to a great disaster. Washington had barely more than fifteen minutes to meet the onslaught of the British forces which had faced about and were beginning to move in his direction. Even in that brief period, however, his masterly qualities as a general were demonstrated. Hastily calling to Wayne, who had just come up, he ordered him to take two regiments and check the assault of the enemy. These troops were drawn up in an orchard flanked on either side by hills, upon which artillery was quickly mounted, to enfilade the advancing British. Under Wayne's command at this time were three regiments of the Pennsylvania Line, one from Maryland and another from Virginia. These sufficed to hold the position until the main body of the army, summoned from the rear by Washington, had arrived. They met the rushes of the English grenadiers, the best regiments in the service, first from the right of Wayne's position, then from the left, but were repulsed on both attempts by the withering volleys of musketry and the constant fire of the field guns.

Then came the most dramatic event of the terrible day. The "crack" regiments of the Guards were brought up, a corps renowned for bravery, dash and perfect discipline, and ordered to charge the American position. Their line was drawn up within a short distance of Wayne's front, and their Colonel, Henry Moncton, a brother of Lord Galway, and one of the most conspicuous and brilliant of the young aristocrats sent out to crush the "vile rebels" of America, as the English contemptuously termed those whom we call "patriots," delivered a stirring and eloquent address, appealing to their soldierly pride, their *esprit de corps,* their loyalty to the King, and other high and noble sentiments. He then commanded them to advance and carry the position at the point of the bayonet, and he himself, with courage worthy honor and renown, led them against the ragged men who had suffered the torments of hunger, cold and exposure, while he was safely housed in the hospitable city of Philadelphia. By all calculations of human probability, these splendid soldiers should have driven the "embattled farmers" in confusion before them, and discouraged the advance of reënforcements from the American rear. They advanced at double quick, a formidable and terrifying array, confident of easy victory, and keyed to the uttermost in the performance of their duty. Wayne's men, who had heard almost every word of the Colonel's stirring speech and at least had seen his gestures, stood their ground, waiting until their would-be assailants were nearly upon them, and then opened their fire with murderous effect. The gallant British Colonel had made his last appeal on earth: he fell riddled with bullets, his face to the foe. Scores of his veterans fell around him, and still the Americans kept up their fire, dropping six men out of every ten at the murderously short range, and throwing the survivors into a confused rout. Some of the more intrepid, with touching bravery, tried vainly to advance far enough to rescue their commander's crumpled body, but even they could not weather the awful hail of the American musketry, and, at last, they were all gone, save only the dead and the desperately wounded, who could not move.

While Wayne's men were holding back the determined assaults of the British, Washington had had time to reform his army, and was advancing all along the line. A fierce cannonade was kept up on both sides, and many assaults were made upon the American positions, but the final result was that the British turned and fled at all points, leaving nearly 1,500 dead and wounded on the field.

Wayne's stand at Monmouth is one of the heroic events of history. It has been compared to the stand of the Greeks at Thermopylæ, and is scarcely less conspicuous. In both cases a mere handful of brave and determined patriots withstood the seasoned warriors of a powerful army, their superiors in nearly every particular except in courage and steadfastness. In both cases, also, they repulsed their assailants with heavy losses, and with every circumstance of humiliation. Seldom has a warlike achievement been more enthusiastically acclaimed by all

110

parties. Wayne became an idol with the people as he had always been among his troops. Only one voice among them all was raised in criticism of his performance, and that was the voice of General Charles Lee, who attempted to clear himself of the serious charge of disobeying orders by arguing the "temerity and folly, and contempt of orders of General Wain" [for so he spelled the name in his letter to Robert Morris], who, as he alleged, had audaciously provoked a battle with "the whole flower of the British army . . . amounting in all to 7,000 men." According to popular understanding of his orders, Wayne and Lee had been expressly commanded to do something closely resembling this very thing. Nor was Wayne guilty of any breach of discipline, as we must insist, even though, in Lee's words, his "folly" was manifested "in the most extensive plain in America, separated from our main body the distance of eight miles."

What Wayne began, rashly or not, on the plains of Monmouth, he and his men were amply prepared to complete, and they did complete it. As he wrote to Richard Peters some two weeks after the engagement:

"The victory of that day turns out to be much more considerable than at first expected. . . . By the most moderate computation their killed and wounded must be full fifteen hundred men of the flower of their army. Among them are numbers of the richest blood of England. Tell the Philadelphia ladies that the heavenly, sweet, pretty Red Coats, the accomplished gentlemen of the guards and grenadiers have humbled themselves on the plains of Monmouth. The Knights of the Blended Rose and Burning Mount have resigned their laurels to *rebel* officers, who will lay them at the feet of those virtuous daughters of America who cheerfully gave up ease and affluence in a city for liberty and peace of mind in a cottage."

Even in the midst of his triumph, Wayne was still the humorist and the solicitous commander. To this spirited epistle he adds the following postscript: "We have not received the least article of clothing since you saw us at Mount Joy, and are now—naked."

CHAPTER X

THE CLIMAX—STONY POINT

WHILE the Americans had decidedly the best of the day at Monmouth, and while the moral effect of the battle was excellent, the results were otherwise small. No booty was captured from the vast British baggage train, and the army was not turned back from its advance on New York. All that the American army could do after its victory was to hang on the rear of the enemy, and, after he had gained his haven in New York, to so dispose the lines that any attempt to advance on the country to the north, on the west bank of the Hudson, could be effectually checked. In the midst of this irksome idleness, during the succeeding summer and autumn months, Wayne again renewed his attempt to persuade Congress and the authorities of Pennsylvania to send the needed supplies to the soldiers. The results were as unsatisfactory as formerly, however—a plethora of large promises and a vacuum of practical performance. Finally, in March, 1779, he succeeded in effecting the passage of a law by Congress giving officers half pay for life; exempting from taxation all land held by soldiers during their lifetime, and, wonderful to relate, providing that they should receive a suitable uniform while in the service.

Wayne, however, was too zealous in the service, too bold in his demands, too entirely devoted to the welfare of the men under him. Such a man as he could be requited only with the highest honors, or merely passed over with mere mention. The latter was the fate of Wayne, the indefatigable commander, the brave soldier and the real victor of Monmouth. As a part of the "new arrangement" of the Pennsylvania Line in February, 1779, he was quietly, even contemptuously, superseded in his command by General Arthur St. Clair, who was best known to his contemporaries as the man who had—needlessly, as it was alleged—evacuated Fort Ticonderoga, and to posterity as the "most unfortunate officer in the Revolution." This was, of course, an occasion of the greatest chagrin to Wayne, who was so angered and disappointed that he actually contemplated for a time resignation from the army and return to civil life. His patriotism and better judgment, however, finally persuaded him to ask only for a leave of absence until his services should be required to command a new corps of the army. During his period of retirement he busied himself in pleading the cause of the army with the government, and in securing such benevolent legislation as has been mentioned in the recognition and rewards of both rank and file.

On Wayne's retirement from the army on leave of absence, General Washington had promised to secure his appointment as commander of a Light Infantry Corps, then in contemplation. This corps might seem to have been organized expressly for Wayne, and its officers and men picked expressly because qualified to serve under him in his daring military movements. On the announcement, in May, 1779, that he was to command this corps, a large proportion of the field officers of the Pennsylvania Line earnestly solicited permission to be transferred to it. So numerous were petitions of this nature that Wayne wrote to Washington, "I had better be absent while the corps is being organized, lest it be supposed, however erroneously, that partiality of mine for certain officers had tended to bring them into the corps."

Wayne assumed command of this newly formed body in the latter part of June, 1779, scarcely three weeks before the momentous exploit in the capture of the fort at Stony Point, with which his name will be forever associated. In this corps were one and one-half battalions of Pennsylvania troops, with two regiments from Connecticut and one from Virginia. In the words of Colonel Francis Johnston, in a letter to Wayne, the command was "preferable to that of any in the army." Excellent as the personnel was declared to be, and, indeed, as it showed itself to be, it could be no more than worthy of its gallant commander. He had made himself a new Leonidas in the orchard at Monmouth, and was destined to make even greater history in the famous surprise and capture of Stony Point.

The fortified post of Stony Point was on the west side of the Hudson River to the south of West Point, and directly opposite to Verplanck's Point, on which was another fortification. The position was upon a rocky promontory 150 feet in height, surrounded on all sides by water, when the tide was high, and access from land was possible only through a stretch of mud flats, when the tide was out. The British had gained possession of it early in June, and had greatly strengthened its defenses, as a preliminary to a determined onslaught upon West Point. Indeed, the possession of West Point, then regarded as the most important fortress in America, was so strongly desired by the British that Howe and Burgoyne had attempted to make a junction, with the view of investing it, in 1777, and, now, the occupation of Stony Point and Verplanck's had been accomplished as a move in a new and well-projected campaign. The defeat of Burgoyne at

Saratoga had destroyed the British hopes in 1777, and the capture of the position by Wayne again thwarted them. They made but one more attempt, when, in the following year, they succeeded in corrupting General Benedict Arnold, whose proposed surrender was prevented only by the capture and subsequent execution of Major John André, a talented man, capable of better things and worthy a nobler end.

It is decidedly indicative of Washington's strong confidence in Wayne's soldierly abilities that he waited impatiently for the latter's return to the army that he might entrust him with the hazardous undertaking of an attempted surprise on Stony Point. Certain it is that Wayne had not been many days installed in his new command before he was at work upon his plans for the attack. Both Wayne and Washington carefully examined the position, and took into consideration every possible plan for entering the fort with the smallest loss of men. A general assault that day would have been out of the question, since the position was amply fortified against the fire of any artillery then in use, and could be approached near enough for an attempt at assault by infantry in mass only after a most appalling loss of life. The plan adopted, therefore, was that Wayne, with a picked body of men, should attempt a surprise attack.

So we come to the night of July 15, 1779, when the surprise attack was made, and the capture of the fort accomplished. Every detail of the work was carefully mapped in advance, nothing had been forgotten or overlooked. The troops, drawn up into separate parties, each with its own particular duty to perform, were fully informed. There were three columns in all. Two were advance columns consisting of 150 picked men, one to work up to the fort on the left side from the land, the other, on the right side; each of them preceded by a "forlorn hope" of twenty tried and trusty volunteers, destined to swift death or lasting renown. These detachments were to prepare the way for their more numerous supporters by clearing away the *abatis*, dispatching or capturing the pickets, and finding the paths over which the remainder could move in approaching the formidable works. The third party was to charge up the slope in the center, and, as the others reached given indicated points, to open a tremendous fusillade, with a view to drawing the fire of the defenders, and thus covering the advance of the surprise detachments on either hand. The left-hand column was commanded by Major Jack Stewart, of Maryland, the right-hand by Colonel Louis Fleury, a French officer in the American service, who was supported by the column under command of Wayne himself. The center was under Colonel Murfrees, of North Carolina.

The attacking corps marched from their camp near New Windsor to Stony Point, a distance of fourteen miles, after dark, arriving in time to open the attack at 11:30 o'clock. The way was wholly along unkempt country roads, upon which the men were often obliged to march in single file. Utter silence was commanded as the prime requisite, and the men were forbidden to drop out of the ranks on any pretext whatever. Wayne was still the exacting disciplinarian, who sternly required literal obedience to the military law. In his address to the men of the Light Infantry, on assuming command, he had said:

"Should there be any soldier so lost to a feeling of honor as to attempt to retreat a single foot, or skulk in the face of danger, the officer next to him is immediately to put him to death, that he may no longer disgrace the name of a soldier, or the corps, or the State, to which he belongs." Nor can we doubt that he gave precisely similar directions to these same men on this, the most momentous evening of his career.

All the precautions were well timed to effect a successful issue. The British, in a calm sense of perfect security, believing that the fort could be assaulted only by a front attack, enfiladed by their cannon, had retired for the night, after posting only the usual number of guards. No one had heard or seen the advancing Americans, who were already on the slopes below the work even before the pickets had detected their advance guards. The attacking column on the right, under Colonel Christian Febiger, and General Wayne, were obliged to wade through deep water, which considerably delayed their progress. Once they reached the *abatis,* however, the path was quickly cleared, and the advance was rapid. Suddenly, from Murfrees' men, moving up the slope in the center, a noisy and continuous fusillade burst forth, awakening the garrison, who soon began answering the fire with musketry and grape shot. The American advance on the left suffered severely, finding the removal of the obstructions more difficult than did their comrades on the right, and being caught in the midst of a hail of bullets. Seventeen out of the twenty men in their "forlorn hope" were stretched dead or wounded on the ground, and the advance column suffered severely also, before the sally port of the fort was finally gained, and the defenses were at their mercy. The three columns arrived at the door of the fort almost simultaneously, and there began a fierce hand-to-hand fight, in which there was no firing—only cold steel and

" 'Forward, my brave fellows, forward!' "

the steady pressure of an overwhelming mass of men.

Just before entering on the fight, Wayne had written a personal letter to Sharp Delany, whom he addressed as "my best and dearest friend," bidding him an affectionate farewell, as he did not know whether he should breakfast "within the enemy's lines in triumph or in the other world." Even his dauntless spirit was impressed with the awfulness of the situation and the desperate character of the attempt upon which he was about to enter. But in nothing did he show that he was *afraid to die.* About halfway up the laborious slope a musket ball plowed a jagged furrow across his scalp, so narrowly avoiding the infliction of a fatal wound that the gallant General fell stunned and helpless in his tracks. Small wonder that he supposed his end was come, for such a wound is both staggering and keen. But he roused himself to a shout:

"Forward, my brave fellows, forward! Victory is already in your hands!" Then, to those beside him he added:

"If I am fatally injured, carry me within the fort, and let me die there in triumph." Having bound up his hurt, his men lifted him on their shoulders and carried him forward to the top of the rise. The rumor spread quickly that General Wayne had been killed, but the soldiers, far from falling back discouraged, rushed forward all the more eagerly, determined to extort an even heavier penalty in their revenge. In such a moment as this the lust of blood rushes in upon men; they turn blind, deaf and senseless to all save the ecstasy of battle!

Only a few minutes more, and the Americans were within the works driving the defenders before them. It was a slaughter grim and merciless, no firing, no sabering, but the continuous stabbing of the bayonets, thrust and thrust! Sixty-three of the British fell by the bayonet within the fort—precisely the number sacrificed in the Paoli "massacre," a life for a life—before the driven regulars threw down their arms and cried for quarter. Nor were the captors relentless. No foeman begged for mercy who was not spared! And they could afford to be lenient. They were victors! Among the American officers Colonel Fleury was first upon the walls. It was he who lowered the British standard, declaring the fort captured. In his broken English he shouted in the hearing of all, above the noise and turmoil of the fight, "Ze fort is ours."

The advance of the American lines began at 11:30, and at 2, Wayne dispatched a note to General Washington, brief, soldierly, generous, with no reference to his own most painful wound:

"The fort and garrison with Colonel Johnston are ours. Our officers and men behaved like men who are determined to be free."

There were taken with Stony Point 543 prisoners of war. The Americans lost fifteen killed, and forty-three wounded. Of the British an even sixty-three were killed, and many more seriously injured, something like twice that number.

Immediately on capturing the fort the guns were trained on the works on Verplanck's Point and on the British ships in the river. Before morning the river and its shores were clear of British soldiers and sailors.

The reputation of General Wayne's victory at Stony Point was immense. He received congratulations from the most distinguished persons in military and government circles, among them his old enemy Charles Lee, who wrote with what seemed to be evident sincerity:

"I do most sincerely declare that your action in the assault of Stony Point is not only the most brilliant, in my opinion, through the whole course of this war on either side, but that it is one of the most brilliant I am acquainted with in history. Upon my soul, the assault of Schweidnitz by Marshal Loudon I think inferior to it. I wish you, therefore, joy of the laurels you have so deservedly acquired, and that you may long live to wear them."

The American Congress, also, a body so curiously insensible to Wayne's earnest, persistent and long-continued appeals for clothing and supplies for the suffering soldiers, voted him a grand gold medal, inscribed in excellent Latin, after the manner of the times, "Antonio Wayne

Duci Exercitus" ("To Anthony Wayne, Leader of the Army"), and to several of his foremost officers, silver medals to the same effect. Thus was Anthony Wayne received among those whose fame is imperishable.

CHAPTER XI

WAYNE WINS THE DISAFFECTED

DURING the months following the successful assault on Stony Point, Wayne's soldierly qualities were occupied, not in fighting with an armed enemy, but in contending endlessly with official incompetence and negligence, in the vain hope of having his command properly supplied with food and clothing. It seems to have been his evil destiny to be ever embarrassed by these ignoble elements, which, more than hardships, discouraging difficulties, or the opposition of a formidable enemy, served to impede his activities. The nearly unbelievable futility and indifference of the authorities were the only agencies that ever thwarted his dauntless courage. Repeatedly, after earnest, persistent and unselfish efforts in behalf of his men and their welfare, he was obliged to give it up, utterly baffled and discouraged. Even the gallant Light Infantry Corps, whose service at Stony Point had shed a halo of glory on the American arms, were not spared the lofty disdain of the commissary department. Nor did Wayne's indignant protest avail to alter the situation in any particular. Matters progressed in regular order from bad to worse, and by the opening of November, as he reported, one hundred and twenty of his command were shoeless. Nor did this sad condition at all excite official compassion. By the end of December few, if any, of the men had been provided for, as is shown in Wayne's note to Washington on the order of Congress that the Virginia regiment be detached from the Light Infantry Corps and proceed to Philadelphia. His reply was brief and to the point:

"Colonel Febiger will march tomorrow at 8 A. M., but for want of shoes he must carry a great many of his people in wagons."

As if it was the opinion of the authorities that the only way to silence the protests of so persistent a protester as Wayne was to be rid of him, the next move was the disbandment of the corps itself. Accordingly, within **four** weeks from the departure of Febiger's men, Wayne again found himself without a command. On February 4, 1780, he wrote to Washington asking that he might be employed in any capacity he might think proper, and then returned to his home in Chester County, Pennsylvania, again compelled to wait patiently and submissively for another opportunity to serve his country with his splendid talents. For nearly fourteen weeks he led the life of a private citizen, presumably caring for his farm and other properties, while waiting eagerly for the summons to return to the service of his country. It came at last, a brief letter from General Washington, containing the strong tribute: "I shall be very happy to see you at camp again, and hope you will, without hesitation, resume your command in the Pennsylvania Line."

Probably Wayne was as happy to be back in camp as was Washington to have him there, but little of importance occurred during the campaign of 1780 that could excite the ardor of even the keenest soldier. Washington's army confined itself principally to watching the movements of the British forces at New York, and to guarding the country between that city and West Point on the north. A few skirmishes occurred, an unsuccessful attack on a Britsh block house—which was celebrated in a series of highly satirical stanzas from the pen of the unfortunate Major André—but for the most part mere marchings and counter-marchings, patrolling the country, and awaiting a decisive move by the enemy. Thus, during the summer and early autumn, did the time pass tediously along. Then came a really momentous event, the capture of the same witty and unfortunate Major André, and the revelation of Arnold's tremendous treasonous plot, which through Washington's quick action was effectively thwarted. For a time, during the exciting weeks following this event, there was plenty to do in the way of guarding positions and preparing to head off expected movements of the enemy, but no fighting. In fact, if we may judge by the records of the time, the whole army came near to perishing of simple ennui.

THE HERO OF STONY POINT

In the midst of the tiresome inaction of the year Wayne experienced all over again the constant annoyances due to the maladministration at the hands of the pompous incompetents who held control of the affairs of his state. There was no improvement worth mentioning in the food problem, nor in the clothing problem, perennially before the eyes of the General. But, added to this, there was a growing spirit of discontent in the Pennsylvania Line. Officers complained that they had not received the recognition and promotions due to their services, nor yet the pay sufficient to the demands of their positions. The men protested that they were sparingly fed, wretchedly clothed—or unclothed—paid only in currency that was either so depreciated as to represent merely a fraction of its face value, or to be utterly worthless in purchasing necessities, and that they were compelled to continue serving long after the expiration of their times of enlistment. Discontent seems to have been still further aggravated by the unwise policy of Congress in appointing to responsible commands men who had seen little or no service in the war, over the heads of seasoned veterans who had worked and suffered unremittingly in the cause of freedom. A notable occasion for protest was the appointment of a certain William Macpherson, a native of Philadelphia, and at the beginning of the Revolution an adjutant in the British service, to the rank of major by brevet. This was in 1779, but in the following year the folly was consummated by the detailing of this officer to the Pennsylvania Line with his brevet rank. The result was that the officers of the Line, with an almost complete unanimity, threatened to resign from the service, and letters of protest were addressed by Wayne and Irvine to General Washington. Macpherson himself seems to have been as unwise and precipitate as his sponsors, for he took part in the controversy by addressing a semi-contemptuous letter to Wayne, bidding him, in effect, to "keep his hands off." The matter was finally settled only by discontinuing the formation of the new Light Infantry Corps, to which Macpherson had been appointed.

All such occasions of discontent led finally to the famous and dramatic incident known as the "Revolt of the Pennsylvania Line." Wayne himself, fully aware of the justness of the protests on nearly every point, was keenly apprehensive of the consequences that must follow persistent inaction, when, on the first of January, 1781, the enlistments of most of his men were due to expire. According to his habit, he wrote letters of warning, protest and advice to President Reed of Pennsylvania, and others who should have helped him in the extremity, had they so chosen. To Reed he writes: "Our soldiers are not devoid of reasoning faculty, nor callous to the first feelings of nature. They have now served their country for nearly five years with fidelity, poorly clothed, badly fed, and worse paid. I have not seen a paper dollar in the way of pay for more than twelve months."

When, even at this crisis, the inertia of the Government could not be neutralized, private philanthropy took up the cause of the soldiers. Several prominent ladies of Philadelphia, under the leadership of Mrs. Sarah Bache, wife of

Richard Bache, then postmaster-general, and the only daughter of Benjamin Franklin, purchased cloth and superintended the manufacture of the sorely needed and much-asked-for clothing. Mrs. Bache collected large sums for this cause by personal solicitation among her wealthy friends, and at one time had as many as 2,200 women constantly at work sewing on the clothing thus paid for. But, as is too often the case with philanthropic efforts, these services were rendered too late to prevent the final grand explosion of the fury that had been smoldering for months in the breasts of the suffering soldiers.

The storm broke on the evening of January 1, 1781, when the men of the Pennsylvania Line, almost without exception, rushed from their squalid quarters, formed under arms on the parade ground, disarmed, although without animosity, disregarded all officers who attempted to interfere with their lawless movements, and proceeded to possess themselves of ammunition, food supplies, horses, and other desirable equipments, including two pieces of artillery.

Wayne, accustomed to quelling mutinies, and given to measures of severe discipline, even when in full sympathy with his men, rushed forward fearlessly, pistol in hand, and ordered an immediate dispersal. The only answer to his command was the presentation of a dozen bayonets at his breast and the stern words of the mutineers' spokesman:

"We love you, we respect you, but you are a dead man if you fire! Do not mistake us: we are not going to the enemy; on the contrary, were they now to come out, you would see us fight under your orders with as much resolution and alacrity as ever." The mutineers then broke camp, and started on their march to Philadelphia, carrying along with them, although without compulsion, General Wayne himself, and Colonels Richard Butler and Walter Stewart. The southward march was attended by no acts of lawlessness or depredation, and was made, as one contemporary has said, "with an astonishing regularity and discipline."

To the inhabitants of Philadelphia, especially

to the members of Congress, awake at last to the consequences of their persistent neglect of the faithful soldiers fighting for freedom, the day of reckoning seemed at hand. Even Washington, who was prevented solely by the necessities of his position from taking severe measures to quell the insurgents, seems to have considered the affair as of the utmost significance. He wrote, some weeks later:

"The weakness of this garrison, and still more its embarrassment and distress from want of provisions, made it impossible to prosecute such measures with the Pennsylvanians as the nature of the case demanded, and while we were making arrangements, as far as practicable, to supply these defects, an accommodation took place which will not only subvert the Pennsylvania Line, but have a very pernicious influence upon the whole army."

The British authorities were, of course, elated at the "revolt," and confidently expected that the mutineers would quickly come over to their lines. Indeed, messengers were sent to meet them from Sir Henry Clinton's camp near

Elizabethtown, New Jersey, offering them most favorable terms to join the British army. The messengers were roughly handled, and confined as spies, while their letters were brought to Wayne himself, with full assurance that, in the event of an attack, they would submit to his command, in order to sufficiently punish those who had suspected them capable of "becoming Arnolds," as their saying was.

Wayne must have been perfectly well aware that the aims of his disaffected troops included no designs for treasons or treacherous violence. But the members of Congress were painfully apprehensive lest they should occupy the city of Philadelphia, and compel the passage of laws for the relief of their distress; they could not disabuse their minds of the conviction that the affair would result in bloodshed. Consequently, a committee, including President Joseph Reed himself, was delegated to meet the soldiers at some point distant from the city, and to treat with them upon their demands. On the way most of the committee lost courage to face these men whom, in their swollen pride, they had contemptuously neglected for so long a period, and Reed, who seems to have had the virtue of courage to offset any defects in his character, proceeded alone to meet the men in their camp near Princeton. Here conferences were held, the demands of the soldiers seriously considered, and the whole affair concluded by a tardy justice, on the one hand, and a loyal submission to authority, on the other.

In their final form, the agreements were:

1. No more enforced service after the expiry of terms of enlistment; also an immediate discharge for all who enlisted under compulsion.

2. The appointment of a board to pass on the question whether an enlistment was for three years only, or for the period of the war.

3. The acceptance of the $100 bounty from Congress on reënlistment not to constitute evidence of enlistment for the whole war.

4. Auditors to be appointed at once to settle the matter of soldiers' pay.

5. Clothing for all men found entitled to a discharge.

6. General amnesty and oblivion.

The result of the examination made by the Commission is well expressed in a letter from Wayne to General Washington, as follows:

"The Commissioners of Congress have gone through the Settlements of enlistments of the Pennsylvania Line, except a few stragglers, and have ordered about 1,250 men to be discharged out of the aggregate of the infantry (2,400 men), and 67 of the artillery, so that we may count upon nearly 1,150 remaining."

Later he wrote:

"We shall retain more than two-thirds of the troops. The soldiers are as impatient of liberty as they were of service."

Beyond doubt, Wayne's presence with the mutineers restrained them from such acts of violence as the less worthy among them might have counseled. The love and respect of his soldiers for him personally—although some complained bitterly that "they had experienced more restraint and strict duty than usual in winter"—undoubtedly led them to submit willingly, after their indubitable wrongs had been righted. Washington was not tardy in recognizing these facts. Indeed, he wrote in a letter to Wayne, at the conclusion of the affair: .

"I am satisfied that everything was done on your part to produce the least possible evil from the unfortunate disturbance in your line, and that your influence has had a great share in preventing worse extremities. I felt for your situation. Your anxieties and fatigues of mind amidst such a scene I can easily conceive. I thank you sincerly for your exertions."

CHAPTER XII

LEADING UP TO YORKTOWN

IMMEDIATELY after the settlement of the mutiny of the Pennsylvania Line, the work of reorganization was begun. Of the 1,250 men discharged by the Commission of Congress, very many reënlisted at once, so that, as Wayne stated confidently, "more than two-thirds of the troops" were immediately enrolled. This matter satisfactorily settled, Wayne wrote to General Washington asking that he be assigned to active field duty, rather than to recruiting. Washington's reply was that active service was then "not possible," although Wayne was excused from the arduous duties of recruiting.

Wayne's return to active service in the field was not long delayed. On February 26, 1781, he was ordered to take a detachment of the Pennsylvania Line, and reënforce General Greene, then operating in South Carolina. His corps, consisting of six regiments, about eight hundred men, had their rendezvous at York, Pennsylvania, and were expected to march in the near future. From various causes, including not only inclemency of the weather, but also the usual preposterous delays about arming and equipping the soldiers, the detachment did not march until after the middle of May. Even with the lesson of the recent mutiny fresh in their memories, the authorities still insisted in paying off the men in the depreciated, almost worthless currency, against which they had formerly protested so strongly. This excited the fury of certain malcontents, who cried out against it on parade, with the result that, in order to nip the tendency to revolt in the bud, they were immediately tried, sentenced and shot before the assembled troops.

Wayne's corps did not march from York until May 20. By that date Cornwallis had already withdrawn his army from South Carolina, and was proceeding northward, to make a junction with the forces under General Phillips on the James River in Virginia. Wayne was now ordered to reënforce General Lafayette, then leading the sole American troops in Virginia, and to do his best in heading off the raiding parties constantly sent out by the enemy to prey upon the surrounding country. While engaged upon this duty Wayne and Lafayette were further ordered by General Washington to prevent, if possible, the retreat of Cornwallis into North Carolina. With this double purpose in view, the two generals constantly hung upon the rear of the British, annoying them as much as possible, while avoiding a general engagement, for which they were not in sufficient numbers nor sufficiently well equipped.

The persistent plan of rear-guard fighting was carefully adhered to at all times, the only exception, and the nearest approach to a general engagement, being at Green Spring, where an attack was attempted under an entire misapprehension of the enemy's strength. On July 6 Lafayette learned from his spies that the British were crossing the river, in order to send columns down on both banks on the way to Portsmouth. According to the understanding given him, Lafayette supposed that by far the larger portion of the enemy's forces had crossed to the opposite shore, leaving only a small part exposed to the attacks of the Americans. Wayne was sent at once to reconnoiter the position, with a force of about 800 men, but, on coming up with the enemy, he found that by far the greater force was still opposed to him, and that he was several times outnumbered. In approaching the enemy the small American force had been obliged to cross a marsh, which was passable only by a narrow causeway. Retreat was, therefore, impossible, and nothing remained but to make such showing as they were able until the arrival of reënforcements from the camp five miles to the rear.

The action began, and continued for some hours, by a constant and "galling" fire of Wayne's riflemen. Finally, at five o'clock in the evening, the British lines began to advance. This was the signal for a spirited attack by Major Galvan, a French officer in the American service, who maintained a gallant fight, until driven back by the British columns. With the

arrival of a small detachment of infantry, under
Major Willis, at this juncture, a heavy fire was
resumed by the Americans, and was continued,
until it was evident the British were preparing
to surround them. Wayne, perceiving that he
was in imminent danger of annihilation or capture, determined on one of the bold moves so
characteristic of his military genius. Having
by this time been strongly reënforced, he determined to save himself by making a sharp and
short attack on the advancing columns, which
should throw them into disorder, thus giving
him the opportunity to withdraw from the trap
and thus prepare for any further movements.
Accordingly, within seventy yards of the British
lines, he opened a furious attack, with both cannon and musketry, which lasted about fifteen
minutes, and served to seriously disconcert his
opponents. In the temporary advantage thus
gained, he withdrew his troops across the
marsh, and reformed on the other side of a piece
of woods commanding the only path upon which
the British could follow him. Although less
spectacular, perhaps, than some of his other

146

notable exploits, this charge served to save his command from envelopment by a force of five times their number, and has been universally praised by military authorities.

After the battle at Green Spring Cornwallis resumed his march to Portsmouth, where he carefully fortified himself, and prepared to make a lengthy stay. Lafayette was afraid, however, that he might use this city as a base for further marauding expeditions, and ordered Wayne to cross the river, and take up a position at a place known as Westover. In this position of vantage he could effectually oppose any attempt to gain the open country in the direction of Norfolk and Petersburg, and, at the same time, would be barred from a retreat into North Carolina.

Thus, these two faithful commanders did their best to carry out the instructions of Washington, but the Commander-in-Chief had other, and even greater objects in view, which included nothing less than the investment and capture of Cornwallis and his entire command. So ably did Washington dissemble his real plans that

Sir Henry Clinton was led to suppose that he intended making an attack on New York, backed by the forces under Rochambeau, then stationed at Newport. Accordingly, with singular fatuity, he ably assisted Washington's real objects by ordering Cornwallis to select the most convenient position near the mouth of the Chesapeake, and there await the coöperation of the British fleet under Admirals Hood and Graves. In giving these commands, he was ignorant, of course, that Washington had information that a powerful French fleet, under Count De Grasse, was on the way from the West Indies, and would enter Hampton Roads late in August, also that another fleet, under Barras, had sailed from Newport to make a rendezvous at the same time. De Grasse's fleet carried 3,000 troops, while that of Barras brought down the heavy siege guns and full stores for the army. Thus, on the arrival of Washington, on September 26, after his wonderful march from New Jersey, the investment of Yorktown was already begun. The combined French fleet engaged the British ships outside the mouth of the Chesapeake, and so disabled them that they could take no further part in the conflict.

There was little opportunity for brilliant and dashing military movements in this affair; nor was any attempted. Wayne's corps was present during the entire period, as a part of the division commanded by Baron von Steuben, taking their part in the daily routine duties of the siege. The situation for Cornwallis was desperate. No resistance was possible that could at all contribute to his relief. Consequently, on the morning of October 19, 1781, he surrendered himself and his entire command prisoners of war.

CHAPTER XIII

IN THE SOUTH

LET us go back to the spring of 1780. General Wayne had been ordered to go South with a detachment of the Pennsylvania Line, 800 strong, and join General Nathanael Greene, then commanding the southern department. In his correspondence Wayne gives as his reason for his failure to advance immediately upon receiving orders that "the troops were retarded in advancing to the general rendezvous (York, Pennsylvania) by the unaccountable delay of the auditors appointed to settle and pay the proportion of the depreciation due the men." The fact is that he was face to face with another mutiny. Later he was delayed by the advance of Cornwallis into Virginia; and so it was not until January 4, 1782, that he and his detachment, consisting of Colonel Butler's, Colonel Walter Stewart's, and Colonel Craig's Battalions of the Pennsylvania Line, and Colonel Gist's Maryland Battalion joined General Greene at Round O, in South Carolina. In the meantime, General Greene had won the battle at Eutaw Springs, by which, quoting from Wayne again, "The British were cooped up in Charleston till the end of the war."

Immediately following the arrival of Wayne at his camp, General Greene sent him to the aid of Georgia, where a most distressing condition of affairs had come about—not so much as the result of the British operations as the culmination of the bitter partisan feelings that had, for a long time, been rampant between the inhabitants of that state. In the bitter, malignant hatred subsisting between the Whigs and Tories, every man's hand was against his brother; in the background was the common enemy—the Indians; slender protection could be procured for life or property, no matter by whom despoiled. Taxes were not to be collected, and so impoverished was the state's exchequer, that, in 1782, the Legislature of the state passed a law authorizing the governor to seize upon the first ten negroes he could find and sell them, the proceeds to go toward the payment of his salary. The most lamentable outrage, practiced by both Whigs and Tories in their internecine strife, was the custom of putting prisoners to death after surrender.

The only British garrison in Georgia which assumed any proportions was stationed at Savannah. It was composed of 1,300 British regulars, 500 well organized and well armed Tories, any number of Tory refugees, and, in addition to these, several hundred Indian allies. To oppose these Wayne had at his command about one hundred of Moylan's dragoons, three hundred mounted men from Sumpter's brigade, and one hundred and seventy volunteers, the whole totaling 570 men, besides the artillery, which numbered less than one hundred men, practically all raw and undisciplined troops. With this discouraging outlook, it is small wonder that the General's heart cried out for his tried Pennsylvania troops who were retained in South Carolina by General Greene. To the latter he wrote a pathetic but unavailing letter:

"Pray give me an additional number of Pennsylvania troops. I will be content with one battalion of Pennsylvanians. They can bring their own field equipage without breaking in upon any part of the army. I will candidly acknowledge that I have extraordinary confidence and attachment in the officers and men who have fought and bled with me during so many campaigns. Therefore, if they can be spared, you will much oblige me."

In spite of the disadvantages enumerated, General Wayne's forces established themselves at Ebenezer, twenty-five miles up the river from Savannah, and made preparations to isolate this garrison from the rest of the state—and particularly to accomplish its separation from the Indian allies. In the meantime, while his preparations for military activity were being made, Wayne carried his campaign into other quarters by recommending to Governor Martin, of Georgia, that he issue a proclamation offering pardon and protection to the Tories who would join the patriots, and which, by the way, indicated also the scant courtesy that would be extended to the Royalists within the state in the event of the success of the patriot army. It was hoped this would produce salutary effects.

His preparations completed, Wayne at once proceeded to the execution of his arduous task. Crossing the Savannah River, February 19, 1782, he applied himself to the seemingly hopeless task of detaching the Indians from the British service. While near the Ogeechee River, fifteen miles from Savannah, he heard of a number of Creek Indians on their way to Savannah. Promptly dressing a number of his men in British uniforms, he sent them to meet the chiefs, who fell victims to the strategy, and were easily captured. After taking from them the provisions which they were carrying down to Savannah, he pointed out to them the failure of the British, the certainty that the Americans would capture Savannah, and made the request that they remain neutral, adding, however, that if they preferred the hatchet to the olive branch, the Americans were ready to meet them. This done, he sent them home. On the twenty-fourth of February Wayne wrote: "It is now upward

154

of five weeks since we entered the state, during which period not an officer nor soldier has once undressed, except for the purpose of changing his linen, nor do the enemy lay on beds of down.'' This waiting period terminated abruptly on the night of the twenty-first of May, when Wayne encountered the greater part of the Savannah garrison, under General Brown, who had come out to meet a band of several hundred Creeks. Acting upon his maxim, ''that the success of a night attack depends more upon the prowess of the men than their numbers,'' he led his three hundred infantry and one hundred dragoons through forty miles of swamp to the enemy's camp. His vanguard—one-fifth as strong as the British force—charged with such impetuosity that Colonel Brown's whole complement, picked infantry, Hessians, and Tories, were defeated and scattered.

After this action, General Wayne removed his camp to Sharon, five miles in front of Savannah. At one o'clock in the morning his rear guard was attacked by a large body of Creek Indians, who were evidently not impressed with the advantages of remaining neutral and who were under the leadership of Gueristersigo, the most famous of Creek warriors. After a slight recoil Wayne's forces recovered from their surprise and charged with such undaunted valor that the savages were routed and driven into the swamp. Gueristersigo was slain, and in one of his letters relating to this encounter, Wayne relates a dramatic episode which probably has reference to the warrior chieftain. He says: "Such was the determined bravery with which the Indians fought, that after I had cut down one of their chiefs, with his last breath, he drew his trigger, and shot my noble horse from under me." At daybreak, the British appeared, but were driven back to their garrison.

Although the House of Commons had voted against the continuance of the war, in February, 1782, and by proclamation had ordered Savannah, as one of the weaker posts, to be the first evacuated, such was the stubborn disposition of its defenders that only after the success of the operations of the Americans narrated above, could they see the wisdom of evacuating the city.

This they finally did on July 11, 1782. Shortly afterward, the situation of Colonel Greene in South Carolina became critical, and Wayne was ordered to effect an immediate junction with him. This he did in August. The light infantry and legionary corps, which had rendered him such important service in Georgia, were added to his command, and, in the latter part of November, he pushed on toward Charleston. On December 14, 1782, he took possession of this city, the last stronghold of the British in the South.

General Wayne, notwithstanding the sobriquet, "Mad Anthony," had once more proved himself a tactful and diplomatic, as well as brave and fearless leader, and at the end of his Southern campaign he was gratified by the following letter from General Greene:

"Dear Sir:

"I am very happy to hear that the enemy have left Savannah, and congratulate you most heartily on the event. I have forwarded an account thereof to Congress and the Commander-in-Chief, expressive of your singular merit and exertions during your command, and doubt not that it will merit their entire approbation, as it does mine.''

Thus brilliantly closed General Wayne's active campaign in the Revolutionary War, and the only sole command for the conduct of which he had been personally responsible. His exploits in compelling the evacuation of Savannah had won him the admiration of citizens and soldiers alike; he was hailed as a military genius and was referred to ''as incomparable as a general and strategist,'' the hero who had rescued an oppressed people from the harrowing anarchy of internal disorders. The gratitude of the people of Georgia, in spite of the dire poverty of the state and its inhabitants, took a most commendable form, by voting, through their Legislature, 3,900 guineas, with which they purchased a rice plantation and presented it to General Wayne as a practical token of their gratitude, and also, it might be remarked, with the ulterior view of inducing him to become a

citizen of Georgia at the close of the war. We
shall have the opportunity, later, to contrast
the attitude of the State of Georgia with that
of General Wayne's native commonwealth toward the one man who, more than any other,
had given Pennsylvania her greatest share of
glory at this greatest and most critical period
of national history. In referring to this negligence of the State of Pennsylvania to make
suitable acknowledgment as to the worth of
her greatest general, one of Wayne's old comrades in Georgia pungently remarked: "It
gives great satisfaction to the generous souls
among your friends here, to think that the people of more Southern climes have paid some
deference to your merits, and have demonstrated it in a more solid manner than empty
praise. This is an article of no more worth
here than the Continental currency."

CHAPTER XIV

THE END OF THE WAR

WITH the end of the war General Wayne found himself confronted by serious problems. Almost immediately after reaching South Carolina he had found his health seriously impaired; in consequence of the fatigue and exposure to which his strenuous campaigns had subjected him, he fell an easy victim to the malarial infections of the Southern swamps; and never afterward did he regain his full health and vigor. Descriptive of this phase of his life, he wrote his friend, Dr. Rush, a characteristic letter: "My physicians, after trying the powers of almost the whole gamut of materia medica, have directed the substitution of regimen and moderate exercise. . . . Be that as it may, I have this consolation, that neither idleness nor dissipation has so injuriously affected my con-

160

stitution; but that it had been exhausted and broken down, by encountering almost every excess of fatigue, difficulty, and danger, in the defense of the rights and liberty of America, from the frozen lakes of Canada to the burning sands of Florida." He nevertheless continued with the army of the South, taking his share of the labors that fell to the officers of the depleted little band of men. During the winter, he concluded treaties of peace with the Creek and Cherokee Indians, as one biographer remarks, "completing the work that he had begun with the sword." Also he received the allegiance of the disaffected portion of the inhabitants of North and South Carolina, thus ending his work of pacification.

In 1783 General Wayne received a tardy recognition of the extraordinary value of his services to his country by his appointment as major-general by brevet, by Congress on recommendation of the executive council of the State of Pennsylvania. In all the annals of army history there is found no parallel case to the failure to make Wayne a major-general by promotion; and it does not improve one's opinions of the political methods of his day to learn that this signal neglect of a man whom all knew to be one of the most patriotic and efficient officers of the patriot army was the result of well meant efforts on the part of Congress to avoid incurring jealousy on the part of the states which had furnished the greatest number of men for the field. Pennsylvania had a sufficient quota of men in service to entitle her to three major-generals, but since a part of them were dispersed on the frontiers, this state had but two commissions; one of these was held by General Mifflin, and the other by General St. Clair, both of whom, it must be admitted, had claims to political influence. Had there been a third commission, its holder would undoubtedly have been Anthony Wayne. Certainly, it is curious to note that, although there was no dissenting voice as to General Wayne's skill as a strategist or record for personal bravery, Congress was compelled by political necessity to withhold from him all public recognition, until his services had been of so conspicuous a nature that to have longer withheld his commission would have been a national scandal.

About this time, too, much unpleasantness and actual sorrow overtook Wayne in connection with his affiliation with and the prominent part he took in the formation of the Society of the Cincinnati, a fraternal association established among the surviving officers of the Revolution for the laudable purpose of aiding each other, and, at the same time, commemorating their valiant deeds. With what seems to have been the characteristic attitude of those who were guiding the helm of state during this critical period of our national life, every effort was made by politicians to discredit the motives of the sponsors of the Society. They were hailed as aristocrats, denounced as the forerunner of the entire loss of national liberty; and some malcontents and hot-heads declared it should be possible to disenfranchise every member of the Society—and, if necessary, "to drive every soul of them out of the state." General Wayne, who had borne without complaint all slights to his own personal dignity, as he himself had said, "solely because of his love for his country and his sense of duty," felt keenly the unjust and ungenerous suspicions which were being circulated concerning the good intentions of the patriotic founders of the Society and expressed his sorrowful and indignant, but clear-headed, view of the situation in a letter to his friend, General Irvine. He wrote:

"Dear General: The revolution of America is an event that will fill the brightest page of history to the end of time. The conduct of her officers and soldiers will be handed down to the latest ages as a model of virtue, perseverance and bravery. The smallness of their numbers, and the unparalleled hardships and excess of difficulties they have encountered in the defense of their country, from the coldest to the hottest sun, places them in a point of view hurtful to the eyes of the leaders of the factions and parties who possess neither the virtue nor the fortitude to meet the enemy in the field, and seeing the involuntary deference paid by the people to the gentlemen of the army,—envy, that green-eyed monster, will stimulate them to seize with

164

avidity every opportunity to depreciate the merits of those who have filled the breach and bled at every pore." Again he descants upon "Caitiff" ingratitude, going back for his precedents to the story of Greece and Rome, and possibly to the early teachings of his Uncle Gilbert.

General Wayne's solicitude for his men did not end with the war, and his anxiety that the return of his soldiers to civil life should be made as easy and simple for them as possible was yet another source of friction between his ideas and those of the government of the state. On April 20, 1783, he wrote President Dickenson, the governor of Pennsylvania, the following letter: "You are pleased to ask my advice on anything respecting the troops under my command belonging to the state. . . . I fondly flatter myself that the wisdom and justice of the Executive and Legislative bodies of Pennsylvania will receive the returning soldiers with open arms and grateful hearts, and I cannot entertain a doubt that they, on their part, will cheerfully and contentedly resume the garb and habits of the citizen.'' What must have been his feeling in regard to the disgraceful occurrence which accompanied the discharge and disbanding of his beloved Pennsylvania troops!

In June, 1783, the soldiers of the American army received a six months' furlough, and, a definite treaty of peace having been agreed upon in the meanwhile, they were discharged in the following December. The soldiers of the Pennsylvania Line were paid off with notes of a nominal value of twenty shillings each, but which were discounted to one-tenth of that amount; and some recruits from the western counties went in a body to Philadelphia to demand justice, an action concerning which there was an unwarrantable misunderstanding. Without the slightest intention or sign of violence on the part of these troops, some of the members of Congress became alarmed and adjourned to Princeton, alleging that their liberty was threatened by a mob, a statement which failed to win either the sympathy or the credulity of the populace. There was, in truth, small need for disturbance, since the first two companies of Wayne's veterans had just arrived from South Carolina and were quartered in the city barracks. Had the disgruntled recruits, many of whom had never been in the field, really been dangerous, the general's loyalty would have led him to give the authorities any necessary protection.

General Wayne saw the last of his Pennsylvania troops embarked from Charleston, en route to Philadelphia, July, 1783. So shattered was his health by the fever and privations he had undergone, that he was prevented from being a participator in the impressive ceremonies that attended Washington's farewell to his army. Also, he was unable to appear in line with his chief on his triumphal progress through Philadelphia on his way to Mount Vernon. Wayne now settled down on his patrimonial estate in Chester county, and gave the time which he had freely bestowed upon his country to the service of his state.

In 1776 the Constitution of the state of Pennsylvania had created a Board of Censors—a body of men who should be elected once in seven years to review the work of the various branches of the state government; and to determine whether this same government had been well or ill conducted; also they were to make a report of their findings to the people—in all, a most comprehensive program. To this Board of Censors General Wayne was elected late in the year 1783, and he became at once one of its most active members. As the chairman of the committee appointed to ascertain how far the provisions of the Constitution had been carried out by legislation, and in what way, if at all, they had been violated, he made a memorable report. In this he showed his anxiety that, now that peace was restored, conciliatory measures should be adopted and such a course pursued as to make the transition from a state of revolution to a condition of normal citizenship as simple a matter as possible. Among the important measures advised by the committee, of which General Wayne was spokesman, was a report strongly urging the revision of the Constitution for the reasons thus frankly stated:

THE END OF THE WAR

"It is known how in times of danger, the Constitution of 1776 forsook us, and the will of our rulers became our only law. It is well known, likewise, that a great part of the citizens of Pennsylvania, from a perfect conviction that political liberty could never long exist under such a frame of government, were opposed to the establishment of it, and when they did submit to it, a solemn engagement was entered into by its friends, that after 7 years should be expired and the enemy driven from our coasts, they would concur with them in making the wished-for amendments."

On his retirement from the Board of Censors, in 1784, General Wayne was elected to the General Assembly to represent his native county of Chester, serving with distinction during the years 1784-1786. This post found him as active and as aggressive in the interest of justice and humanity as past record had proved him to have been in the performance of any duty to which he was called. His chief desire was to make the Revolution and its results a source of blessing to all, and with this in view, his efforts were mainly directed to the unification and general satisfaction of all who made up the body politic of the state. In this endeavor, his attention was necessarily directed to the notorious "test laws" of Pennsylvania, passed in 1777 and 1778, and which disenfranchised forever, as *suspected,* Tories, Royalists, and others who had refused, before November, 1779, to take the oath renouncing allegiance to the King of Great Britain and declaring fidelity to the state of Pennsylvania. Among those to whom this law bore great hardship were the Quakers, who from religious scruples were opposed to all political tests, and who formed the most praiseworthy part of the state. In all, these acts affected nearly one-half of the population of Pennsylvania—if the amount of taxable property be taken into consideration, more than that—and those who refused to subscribe were declared incapable of electing or being elected, or holding any place under the government, they were precluded from serving on juries, keeping schools, except in private houses, and forever excluded from taking said oath afterward.

THE END OF THE WAR

By reason of his distinguished military career, General Wayne was particularly adapted to the task of amending this grievance to the citizens of his state, and here, as elsewhere, he showed himself a fearless and persistent fighter. His first petition asking for the abandonment of these "tests," presented in March, 1784, was defeated. In September, and again in December, propositions made by General Wayne were voted down, a committee reporting on the latter occasion, "that it would be impolitic and dangerous to admit persons who had been inimical to the sovereignty and independence of the state to have a common participation in the government so soon after the War." A bit of sophistry as short-sighted as it was lacking in ingenuity. The struggle began in 1784 and continued until 1789, when a motion was adopted to repeal all laws requiring any oath or affirmation of allegiance from the inhabitants of the state.

In 1787 General Wayne was a member of the Convention called in Pennsylvania to ratify the Constitution of the United States, and it is need-

less to say that he was one of the most ardent
supporters of its adoption. His distinguished
public career had, however, for a long time
been harassed by the unfortunate state of his
domestic concerns. By the year 1790 it was
clear to all that the brave and resourceful general was a very poor business man—if success
meant the ability to compete with the money-
makers of his time. It was a disgraceful period,
when low, thievish methods of transacting business were looked upon with the greatest indul-
gence. Also, the sanguine nature which had
been one of his most valuable characteristics in
enheartening his soldiers and bringing his military campaigns to a victorious end, became in
private life his most serious drawback; and with
the fatality which seemed to attend him, the
plantation in Georgia, with which its citizens
had presented him with such good intentions,
now became the source of his deepest unhappi-
ness and humiliation.

He had devoted much of his time since his
return from the army to the rehabilitation of
his handsome patrimonial estate in Chester

county, which had suffered severely in the hands of the agents in whose hands he had been obliged to commit his interests during his long absence in his country's behalf. In the meantime, he was seeking to devise a means by which his rice plantation in Georgia could be made productive. This could not be managed without the purchase of slaves to a considerable number, and for this outlay he did not have the means. Someone, probably his friend Robert Morris, suggested to him that he negotiate a loan for that purpose in Holland. Acting upon this hint, Wayne wrote the Minister Resident of Holland in this country, Mr. Van Berkle, a letter wherein he set forth the nature of his security and his needs in picturesque terms that bear unmistakable evidence of the integrity with which he expected to carry out his share of the bargain. After some formal information as to location, etc., he says:

"The estate used to net Sir James Wright from 800 to 1,000 guineas per annum—it is therefore an object of considerable consequence to me to set to work again as soon as possible, for which purpose I shall proceed for that Quarter in the course of a few weeks in order to prepare it for a crop in the Spring, but I shall want the aid of about 4,000 guineas to stock it with negroes.

"I will punctually pay the Interest by annually remitting rice to Amsterdam, altogether with the principal in the course of two or three years."

It is a sad commentary on the state of our national credit at the beginning of our history as a united people that neither in this country nor in Europe could one of America's greatest military heroes borrow four thousand guineas on the security which included both his Georgia plantation and his Pennsylvania estate. Unfortunately it did not occur to the general that such a state of things could exist, and thinking the loan concluded, he drew bills for that amount on his correspondents, probably, as evidence goes to show, using the whole amount for the purchase of negroes. The bills fell into the hands of a Scotch agent in Savannah who demanded immediate payment. After many difficulties and embarrassments, Wayne was ultimately obliged, in order to save his patrimonial estate, to sacrifice his Georgia property. In full justice to him let it be here said that he had made this proposition in the beginning of the controversy, and that the only answer to this was a suit in law, the only object of which was to make both his estates liable for payment.

In 1890, although it was quite apparent that all hope of his becoming a resident of Georgia, even for a part of the time, as he had intended to do, was past, a large number of his friends there determined that General Wayne should represent them in Congress. Accordingly he was returned as elected on January 3, 1791; but at the instigation of his opponent the House investigated and on March 16, 1792, set forth that "Anthony Wayne was not duly elected a Member of this House." At no time was it ever charged that Wayne had any knowledge of or part in the irregularities charged to his over-zealous friends. His own version of the matter, given soon after the decision of the House, is no doubt the correct one. He says: "Both Federalists and Anti-Federalists pronounced in the halls of Congress, after the fullest investigation, my character stood pure and unsullied as a soldier's ought to be."

After the chagrin attendant upon the unfortunate Georgia controversy, it was small wonder that General Wayne felt an overwhelming desire to go back to military life. In line with this he urged one of his friends, a member of Congress, to petition for his appointment to the command of the forces which his judgment with regard to the dangers that menaced his country convinced him would be needed at no distant date to repel the incursions of the Creek Indians. Only a few days after the question of his Congressional election had been decided President Washington evinced his confidence in him as a man of honor and the foremost military leader of the young Republic by appointing him General-in-Chief of the army.

CHAPTER XV

CALLED BACK TO THE ARMY

THE magnitude of the trust reposed in General Wayne by President Washington can only be understood in the light of the serious conditions prevailing on the Northwestern frontier at the time of General Wayne's appointment. After the cession of the lands north and west of the Ohio River to the United States by Virginia and Connecticut, a territorial government had been formed in that region, by the ordinance of Congress of July 13, 1787—a famous document in American history—and General Arthur St. Clair was appointed governor. Emigrants were offered every inducement, and large bodies of them sought homes in this Northwest Territory. These pioneers lived in constant fear of the savages, for the Indian allies of Great Britain had refused to bury the hatchet when peace was made, some historians

177

claiming that, actuated by the hope of acquiring the Northwest Territory and the Canadas in time, the British had persuaded the red men to fight for their lands. Add to this supposititious case a determination on the part of the savage, quite independent of any quarrel with the whites, that the white man should never occupy the lands west of the Ohio, and the true source of the frequent raiding and scalping parties is apparent. From 1783 to 1790 it was estimated that no fewer than 1,500 settlers, including women and children, had been slain or captured by the Shawnees and Delawares who occupied the region.

These tribes, reinforced by the Wyandottes, the Miamis, the Chippewas and the Pottawato-mies, concentrated near the Miami and the Maumee rivers and Lake Erie. Here they had access to the Indians of the interior, to the Canadians, and the British, who were still holding Detroit and other posts northwest of the Ohio. Both of these latter, no one doubts who searches the records, aided and encouraged the Indians in their forays by the loan of organized forces.

CALLED BACK TO THE ARMY

In January, 1789, Governor St. Clair, finding that he was unable to compel the Indians to stand by their treaties, determined to send a military force to the rescue of the helpless frontiersmen, and in 1790 General Harmar, who had been one of the most distinguished officers of the Pennsylvania Line, was dispatched to put an end to the Indian atrocities. This army, badly equipped and undisciplined, led by officers who, though they were brave, were lacking in experience in the ways of the wily red man, met the Indians in force at what is now Fort Wayne, Indiana, and, practically annihilated, were forced to retreat to Fort Washington (Cincinnati). The moral effect of this failure was distressing; the savages were only the more incensed and confident in their own prowess, and made their attacks with greater ferocity than before.

General St. Clair himself was now sent to the Northwest with a picked band of men, consisting of 2,300 regular troops. On November 3, 1791, he encamped where Recovery, Mercer County, Ohio, now stands. Here was the man of destiny, and the eyes of the nation were fixed upon him with lively solicitude. The fight began at sunrise of November 4. Regular military tactics failed completely; officer after officer was shot down, until upward of sixty were slain; and when the Indians penetrated the camp of the militia at the end of the line the result was a total rout. Besides the officers enumerated before, 630 soldiers were killed, and of the remaining 1,400 who survived we are told that "scarce half a hundred were unhurt." Altogether it was the most disastrous defeat sustained at the hands of the savages since the historic defeat of General Braddock; and it proved an even greater disaster by reason of the great depression felt by the American people. In this battle were killed many of the most distinguished men in the Pennsylvania Line under Wayne's command, and that leader was also deprived of his heroic and brilliant friend, General Richard Butler.

The dismay and consternation into which these defeats, especially that of General St. Clair, threw the country made capital for the opponents of the administration; while from continued ill success the people looked with disfavor upon a military life as a calling, the only certain reward of which would be to fall by the rifle, the tomahawk, or the scalping-knife, for the Indians were well armed and provided with powder and ball. The cost of maintaining the army in the present low condition of the national treasury was another reason against another campaign; and the many abuses which had crept into the management of the St. Clair campaign—insufficient arms and wretched food. All these things furnished proofs to the public mind of gross misconduct on the part of the administration, and were made liberal use of to accomplish party ends. Congress, however, had sufficient strength to support the President in his views, and by an act approved March 5, 1792, authorized him to reorganize the army.

It can now be readily realized that at this critical juncture the selection of the commanding officer was more important than at any time since the commencement of the Revolution. Washington must risk his own fame, even, in this one act, for failure would mean the most deeply humiliating consequences. A man was needed who possessed sound judgment, the greatest caution and coolness, a broad knowledge of military science; he should be a strict disciplinarian, and, above all, a patriot. Envious officers and statesmen who had the ear of the President constantly represented to him that "Wayne was brave and nothing else"; his unsuccessful business ventures had created an ill impression which his strong integrity had not counterbalanced; and his love of fine clothing and display were vulnerable points of criticism. Nevertheless, Washington found that much-needed man in General Wayne, and appointed him to the command of his expeditionary forces in April, 1792.

The United States army as it was then organized consisted of 5,120 non-commissioned officers and privates, one major-general, four brigadier generals, and their staffs, the whole known as the Legion of the United States. This Legion was to be subdivided into four sub-legions, each to consist of 1,280 non-commissioned men and privates. With this force of men General Wayne set out on his expedition May 24, 1792, stimulated and forewarned by the parting declaration of Secretary of War, General Knox, that "another defeat would be inexpressibly ruinous to the reputation of the Government." Wayne's only stipulation was that the campaign should not begin until his Legion was filled up and properly disciplined, wherein we may see that he put his trust in good management rather than in good fortune.

CHAPTER XVI

FIGHTING THE NORTHERN SAVAGES

GENERAL WAYNE went to Pittsburgh in June, 1792, and straightway began to assemble and organize his Legion. A hard task it was! His recruits were gathered from the slums and prisons of the Eastern cities—the refuse of the nation. Tales of the horrible mutilations inflicted by the Indians and the plentifulness of whisky about Pittsburgh were hardly calculated to inspire these wretched beings with devotion to the cause. Desertions followed to such an extent that the recruits fled in squads, fifty-seven leaving a small detachment on the road to Pittsburgh at one time, and of those who remained Wayne wrote the Secretary of War in a letter dated August 10, 1792:

"Desertions have been frequent and alarming —two nights since, upon a report that a large body of Indians were close in our front, I or-

184

dered the troops to form for action, and rode along the line to inspire them with confidence, and gave a charge to those in the redoubts, which I had hastily thrown up in our front and right flank, to maintain their posts, at the expense of blood, until I could gain the enemy's rear with the dragoons; but such is the defect of the human heart, that from excess of cowardice one-third of the sentries deserted from these stations so as to leave the most accessible places unguarded.''

To add to his difficulties, since so many of his most dependable officers had perished in the disastrous campaigns of Generals Harmar and St. Clair, he was confronted with the necessity of drilling officers as well as privates. For a time he worked as best he could in Pittsburgh, then, on November 28, shipped his recruits, who had been immeasurably improved in discipline and numbers, down the Ohio River to a camp twenty-seven miles below Pittsburgh, which he called Legionville. Here he settled down to a winter of hard work as drill-master.

In the meantime, mindful of his duty to his

Government and the American people, Wayne had left no stone unturned to ascertain the disposition of the Indians towards peace. He made every effort to impress them with the earnest desire of the United States to accept any terms that would be just and honorable. In answer, the Indians continued their depredations on the frontier, and, claiming superiority, sent repeated and boastful messages as to their hopes on seeing the Legion advance into their country. Colonel Harding and Major Truman, who went to them—not, it must be understood, by the order of General Wayne, but from the Government—were received at first with every manifestation of good-will and then foully murdered, despite the fact that they carried flags of truce and were unarmed. Still anxious to conciliate, Wayne sent an invitation to a council to Cornplanter, and other chiefs of the Six Tribes who had been disposed to be friendly. In a dramatic toast given at the general's table, Cornplanter said: "My mind and heart are upon that river"—pointing to the Ohio—"may that water ever continue to run and remain the

boundary of lasting peace between the Americans and the Indians on its opposite shores.''
This sentiment of the ''friendly Indians,'' fanned and sustained by British policy, became the obsession of the hostile tribes, who demanded that the Americans renounce all claims north and west of the Ohio, regardless of treaty or fair purchase. It was, therefore, upon the ground of the protection of unquestionable rights, as well as for the purpose of curbing Indian ferocity, and not from a policy of aggression, that Wayne advanced at last into the country of the savage.

At Legionville, during all that winter, the resourceful and tireless Wayne wrought wonders with his hopeless material. A review of the work he did there gives us a new view—that of thoroughness—of the fastidious Revolutionary general who had ''an insuperable bias in favor of an elegant uniform and soldierly appearance,'' and who was ''determined to punish any man who came on parade with a long beard, slovenly dressed, or dirty.'' He instructed his riff-raff mob in military tactics and duties; more than that, he made men of them, as he marched them up and down the parade grounds. What he accomplished that winter has led one historian to remark: "Anthony Wayne—'Mad Anthony'—was not only an ideal leader of men in time of battle, but he was the most capable drillmaster the American army ever had."

Of the result of his efforts, General Wayne wrote to Secretary Knox, March 30, 1793, "The progress that the troops have made both in maneuvering and as marksmen astonished the savages on St. Patrick's day; and I am happy to inform you that the sons of that Saint were perfectly sober and orderly, being out of reach of whisky, which *baneful poison* is prohibited from entering this camp except as the component part of a ration, or a little for fatigue duty, or on some extraordinary occasion." With characteristic hopefulness he was now inspired with such confidence in the success of his expedition that he solicited the secretary of state to send him "certain legionary distinctive decorations; also a legionary standard, and sub-legionary and battalion colors." On receiving them he wrote: *"They shall not be lost!"*

In May, 1793, General Wayne moved his camp to Fort Washington—the present site of Cincinnati—where he continued his efforts to maintain a well-disciplined force. From the administration and from the prevailing conditions of the time, all adverse to obtaining coöperation and obedience essential to the preservation of an unbroken front, he had small encouragement to pursue his work. In January, 1793, Secretary of War, General Knox, had written:

"The sentiments of the citizens of the United States are adverse in the extreme to an Indian war."

A commission, consisting of three prominent Americans, General Lincoln, Colonel Pickering, and Beverly Randolph, Esq., of Virginia, were sent by the government to treat with the Indians who had indicated a disposition to consider peace; and while these negotiations were pending, Secretary Knox again wrote:

"It will therefore be still more and more necessary even than in the past summer, that no offensive be taken against the Indians.''

Moreover, it is said, that at the instigation of the British who accompanied these peace commissioners, the latter wrote Secretary Knox a strong protest against Wayne's work on the drill-ground, as ''this procedure on his part angered the Indians, and that the *British* considered it unfair and unwarrantable.'' Nevertheless the general's experience with the savages had convinced him that they would not yield, and he persevered in perfecting his army. He was justified in his convictions, for when the peace commissioners reached Detroit, August 13, 1783, they received from a general council the following message:

''Brothers: We shall be persuaded that you mean to do us justice if you agree that the Ohio shall remain the boundary line between us. If you will not consent thereto, our meeting will be altogether unnecessary.''

A battle was now inevitable, if not a prolonged war, and Wayne, who had sent to Kentucky for mounted volunteers while awaiting the end of the negotiations, was ready. At last, in September, 1793, General Knox wrote:

"The Indians have refused to treat . . . every offer has been made to obtain peace by milder terms than the sword; the efforts have failed under circumstances which leave nothing for us to expect but war," continuing with the oft repeated warning, "Let it therefore be again, and for the last time, impressed deeply upon your mind, that as little as possible is to be hazarded, that your force is fully adequate to the object you' purpose to effect, and that a defeat at the present time, and under the present circumstances, would be pernicious in the highest degree to the interests of our country."

To this suggestion General Wayne sent a forcible reply: "I pray you not to permit present appearances to cause too much anxiety either in the mind of the President or yourself on account of the army. Knowing the critical situation of our infant nation, and feeling for the honor and reputation of the government (which I will defend with my latest breath), you may rest assured that I will not commit the Legion unnecessarily.''

Wayne now started on his advance into the Indian country. On October 7 he left "Hobson's Choice," as he called his camp near Cincinnati, with his legions of troops on the march through the wilderness. On October 13, he encamped on a spot which he named Greeneville, in honor of his old friend and comrade, General Greene—a post six miles north of Fort Jefferson and eighty miles from Cincinnati. This place he fortified for his winter quarters, and here the command spent several months cut off from all communication with the government at Philadelphia, and surrounded by hostile savages. There were frequent encounters with these when convoys of provisions were surprised and their escorts murdered. As a means of giving his troops experience, on December 23, Wayne sent several companies of soldiers forward to the battlefield on which St. Clair had met his defeat in 1791, with the double purpose of burying the bones of their comrades who had perished there, and to fortify the site.

FIGHTING THE NORTHERN SAVAGES

In order to encourage the troops who were ordered to this service, Wayne personally advanced to the same spot.

After the erection of this fort, which he named "Fort Recovery," General Wayne received some overtures of peace from the Indians, to whom, although he had no faith in their professions, he expressed himself as highly gratified and agreed to open negotiations, only asking that, as proof of their sincerity, they should deliver to him the captives they had taken. This was never done, and nothing more was heard of pacific proposals. On the contrary, the situation became every day more difficult; it needed the exercise of the widest vigilance and wisdom on the part of the commander of our army and the utmost loyalty of his followers. With the impressment of American seamen, the confiscation of our cargoes, and other hostile acts of the English thus going on, there was every prospect of war with Great Britain. Moreover, the British, who still maintained strong garrisons on the frontier, built a fort at the foot of the Maumee Rapids (Fort

Miami), which the Indians believed to be impregnable and the erection of which no doubt encouraged them to hope that, in case of battle, they would be supported by tried battalions of English allies.

From these circumstances it may be seen that General Wayne's position was such that one injudicious move on his part might certainly be the means of bringing on a second war with Great Britain. In this emergency the prudence of his conduct was such that at last he obtained the tardy approbation of his government. A communication from the Secretary of War, dated March 31, informed him that the way in which he had taken a position on the scene of General St. Clair's defeat, and the manner in which he had treated the false peace proposals of the hostile red men, were "highly satisfactory and exceedingly proper." The secretary proceeded to say:

"It is with great pleasure, sir, that I transmit to you the approbation of the President of the United States for your conduct *generally,* since you have had the command, and more particularly, for the judicious military formation of your troops; the precautions you appear to have taken in your advance, in your fortified camp, and in your arrangements for a full and abundant supply of provisions on hand"—a commendation most flattering in view of the reverses encountered by his predecessors, Harmar and St. Clair. Later, General Knox wrote:

"If therefore, in the course of your operations against the Indian enemy, it should have become necessary to dislodge the party at the rapids of the Miami (meaning the English garrison), you are hereby authorized in the name of the President of the United States to do it."

Thus was "Mad Anthony" Wayne given power to conduct the war according to his sole discretion; also to take the step which might have led to war with England.

Hostilities opened on the morning of June thirtieth, 1794, when, under the walls of Fort Recovery, an escort under Major M'Mahan was attacked by a large body of Indians and driven into the fort, Major M'Mahan and other valued officers losing their lives. An assault was then made on the fort, and the Indians, who were repulsed with heavy loss, gained from their discomfiture some degree of respect for the new American Commander-in-Chief and American arms. About the middle of July General Wayne was joined by a strong mounted force from Kentucky, under the command of Major-General Scott. He now judged his preparations complete and moved up to the English garrison at Fort Miami. Here he constructed a fortification at the junction of the Le Glaize and Miami rivers, which he appropriately called Fort Defiance. Although now fully prepared to strike the blow which would forever settle the question of supremacy on the American frontier, Wayne made one more attempt to secure peace without bloodshed, and sent the Indians a proposition by a special flag. Confident of the assistance promised by their white allies, and secure in their own prowess, the savages rejected all proposals, and one of the most memorable Indian battles in all history followed.

On the morning of the fifteenth of August the army advanced from Fort Defiance; and on the eighteenth arrived at Roche de Bout, at the head of the rapids; they camped there until the nineteenth, while scouts examined the enemy's ground and small fortifications. On the morning of the twentieth the Americans advanced in two lines through a thick wood extending for miles on every side, where the savages lay in wait. The ground of the forest was covered with fallen timbers, the aftermath of a tornado, and the whole situation was an ideal one for the foe. In a location such as this the cavalry were practically useless, while two miles below was the British fort, from which the Indians expected help in extremity. Five or six miles below the camp, Major Price, with his advance guard, saw Indians and charged. Upon that, the enemy in full force in the midst of the tangled tree trunks opened a galling fire that threw the Kentuckians back on Wayne's main army. It was the supreme moment. Wayne now ordered the militia, under General Scott, to turn the enemy's right, and the dragoons of the Legion to cut in between the river and the enemy's left. At the same time the line of infantry, 900 strong, with bayonets fixed, was stretched before the enemy's fighting front; while a second line was placed in the rear as reserve forces. When the word was given to charge, every man leaped forward, yelling with the joy of the fight; they bayoneted the red men and their allies behind the logs, and shot them down as they fled, until they had driven them past the British forts (which were tightly closed) and scattered them in the wilderness. Thus the bayonet charge decided the fate of the battle and practically ended the long warfare on the frontier. A few small raids were afterwards made, but the tribes lost hope of victory. In this engagement the American loss was 33 killed, and 100 wounded. The Indians lost several times as many. The army now returned to Le Glaize by easy marches, reaching that post on the twenty-seventh of August; thence they marched to Fort Defiance and back to Greeneville.

Although suffering acutely from an attack of the gout on the morning the battle began, General Wayne was able to prevail over his physical disability, and spent much of the next day, with his staff, in reconnoitering the British fort, thus giving great offense to the commander, Major Campbell. As the result of this incident the following epistolary exchange of views took place:

"Major Campbell to General Wayne.

"Sir,—An army of the United States of America, said to be under your command, have taken post on the banks of the Miami for upwards of the last 24 hours almost within reach of the guns of this fort, being a post belonging to his Majesty the King of Great Britain, occupied by his Majesty's troops, and which I have the honor to command, it becomes my duty to inform myself as speedily as possible in what light I am to view your approach to this garrison. I have no hesitation, on my part, to say that I know of no war existing between Great Britain and America.

"I have the honor, etc., etc."

Neither did General Wayne have any "hesitation," for he replied to this effect:

THE HERO OF STONY POINT

"Sir:—I have received your letter of this date, requiring from me the motives which have moved the army under my command to the position that they at present occupy far within the acknowledged jurisdiction of the United States.

"Without questioning the authority or the propriety of your interrogatory, I think I may, without breach of decorum, observe to you that you are entitled to an answer. The most full and satisfactory one was announced to you from the muzzles of my small arms yesterday morning in the action against the hordes of savages in the vicinity of your post which terminated gloriously to the American arms, but had it continued until the Indians, *etc.*, were driven under the influence of the post and guns you mention, they would not much have impeded the progress of the Victorious Army under my command—as no such post was established at the commencement of the present war between the Indians and the United States."

CHAPTER XVII

THE GOVERNMENT COMMISSIONER AND CONCLUSION

THE importance of General Anthony Wayne's services in forcing the decisive battle at the Falls of the Miami, which resulted in the complete subjugation of the Indians of the Northwest, cannot be overestimated. He is entitled to lasting fame and to the enduring gratitude of the millions of prosperous people who now inhabit the fertile lands lying between the Ohio and the Mississippi rivers, as the man who opened this magnificent domain to the home-seeker, and obtained for him the constitutional, and *actual,* right to life, liberty, and the pursuit of happiness on his own lands. By the brilliant success of this victory over the combined tribes, the government gained immeasurably in lands and in power; while it was still more far-reaching in aiding the American ambassador, John Jay, in bringing to a reasonable conclusion the terms of the treaty he was negotiating with the English ministry in regard to their retention of garrisons on American soil. The news of this battle reaching London, it was felt that all hope of further aid from the Indians was at an end, and orders were given for the evacuation of the British forts in American territory. Also, the battle of the Miami put an end to vexations arising from a cherished dream of the Spanish authorities that their dominion in America might some day be recovered. Nor must it be forgotten that in the flush of victory, the factions at the national capital were reconciled for a season, and the stain of recent defeats wiped from American arms.

On September 14, 1794, after having accomplished his purpose, General Wayne and his army left Fort Defiance and returned to Greeneville for winter quarters. Preliminary articles were entered into, January 1, 1795, and hostages left with General Wayne for the safe delivery of prisoners in possession of the Indians. Elated at the victory of his commander-in-chief,

"The treaty with the Indians."

THE GOVERNMENT COMMISSIONER

President Washington forthwith issued a commission, appointing General Wayne sole commissioner, with full powers to negotiate and conclude a treaty with all the Indians north and west of the Ohio. In these negotiations General Wayne displayed the same wisdom and prudence, tempered by humanity, that had made him conspicuous as a military leader. He treated the chiefs and warriors with the greatest courtesy and frankness; explained to them the views of the government, and just what it expected of them. In return for their cession of lands they received $20,000 in goods, which were distributed among the Indians present, while another annuity, amounting to $9,500, was granted to the tribes represented. By this straightforward course he gained their confidence and respect. As a last word, he told them that they were "children and no longer brothers." Definite terms of peace were concluded on August 17, 1795, and the Indians returned to their homes well pleased.

The treaty of Greeneville also met the warm approval of the government, for by its terms a vast tract of territory west of the Ohio and northwest to Detroit was ceded to the United States. The lines enclosing the Indian territory were drawn from Lake Erie along the Cuyahoga River to Portage, hence west to the Maumee, down that river to the lake (Erie) and thence to the place of beginning. Within these lines the claim of the Indians to territory was acknowledged, and beyond them lay the land of the whites. By its favorable terms the treaty of Greeneville had thus procured for the government land to the value of millions, and, what is of more importance, a peace which lasted uninterruptedly for seventeen years.

The treaty concluded, General Wayne, who had lived in the wilderness for three years, practically without news of the outside world, returned to Pennsylvania. His progress was that of a conquering hero. On his approach to Philadelphia all business was suspended, and four miles from the city he was met with three troops of light horse. The newspapers of the day give the following account: "On his crossing the Schuylkill a salute of 15 cannon was fired from Centre Square by a party of artillery. He was ushered into the city by the ringing of bells and other demonstrations of joy, and thousands of citizens crowded to see and welcome the return of their brave general, whom they attended to the City Tavern, where he alighted. In the evening a display of fireworks was exhibited." This was his one great day—when all men acknowledged the worth of his work.

President Washington, in a message to Congress, gratefully acknowledged the exploits of General Wayne and the vast consequences likely to follow them and an attempt was made to have fitting acknowledgments made in the House of Representatives. Again party jealousy deprived the general of his just deserts, and the House adopted the following resolution:

"*Resolved Unanimously*, that the thanks of this House be given to the brave officers and soldiers of the Legion under the orders of General Wayne for their prudence and bravery."

During the winter of 1796, opposition to the

enforcement of Jay's treaty had become so violent that the probable refusal of Congress to make the necessary appropriations for carrying it into effect led to the belief that another war with Great Britain was impending, a war loudly demanded by the "Jingoists" of that day. Since the treaty involved the right of the English to retain their fortifications on our frontier, and by holding that vantage ground on American territory they might again seek the alliance of the Indians and involve the Western lands in warfare, it was of the utmost importance that the articles of the treaty be promptly carried out. On April 30, the memorable debate on this bill was concluded, and by a vote of 51 to 48, the House decided to make the appropriation in question, and orders were sent to the British

These measures had been taken just in time, commanders to evacuate their forts.

for news came that the English had been soliciting the aid of the Indians for a new campaign in the Northwest Territory, and at this critical juncture, General Wayne was selected as the one man who could accomplish the delicate and hazardous mission of taking possession of the British strongholds in the name of the United States government. One writer says: "He knew the English on the border, with their allies, the Indians, and they knew him. Moreover, the man who had won the territory was the one to whom the honor of receiving it was due."

Under these circumstances, charged with full discretionary powers, General Wayne was sent, in June, 1796, to the British posts at Detroit, Michelimackinack, Oswego, and Niagara. On his approach the Indians at once became friendly; he was received in the most courteous manner by the English officers in command of the garrisons of the different forts; and in no case did he meet any obstacle in rendering his last great service to his country. He reached Detroit in September, where he was welcomd by demonstrations from the settlers he had saved, and the red men who had been his foe. After remaining for two months at this post, on the seventeenth of November, he sailed from Detroit for Presqu'isle, the site of the present city of Erie, the last station on his itinerary. The day before he landed, he was seized with a violent attack of gout, and was taken ashore in a dying condition.

He was at once removed to the quarters of the commandant of the post, and lay for many days in the most excruciating agony. Surgical skill was unable to reach him, and at last, on December 15, he breathed his last a few weeks before his fifty-second birthday. He was buried, according to his wish, at the foot of the flagstaff on a high hill, called Garrison Hill, north of the site of the present Soldiers' Home. In 1809, Colonel Isaac Wayne caused his illustrious father's remains to be moved and interred in the family burying ground attached to St. David's Church, at Radnor—the same St. David's a writer has thus beautifully described:

"As a place of worship, its location is essentially happy. But not until you are almost upon it, as you approach it is the unobtrusive little sanctuary seen, peeping from among the trees which conceal it from view—thus, as it were, shutting out the world and all those cares and objects not in unison with the feeling of holy meditation. . . . There is, however, in the yard, *one,* at least, whose name fills a conspicuous place in the page of his nation's history—a monument more enduring than brass. The individual alluded to is the late Major-General Anthony Wayne."

In 1876, the empty grave at Erie was discovered, and in 1879, the Legislature of Pennsylvania appropriated $1,500.00 for the erection of a suitable monument on the spot. The committee on erection adopted as a model for the monument which now stands at Erie, the old block-house in which the hero died. The following is the inscription which commemorates his deeds:

MAJOR-GENERAL
ANTHONY WAYNE
BORN AT WAYNESBURGH
IN CHESTER COUNTY
STATE OF PENNSYLVANIA
A. D. 1745
AFTER A LIFE OF HONOR AND USEFULNESS
HE DIED IN 1796,

THE HERO OF STONY POINT

ON THE SHORES OF LAKE ERIE
COMMANDER-IN-CHIEF OF THE ARMY OF
THE UNITED STATES.
HIS MILITARY ACHIEVEMENTS
ARE CONSECRATED
IN THE HISTORY OF HIS COUNTRYMEN.
HIS REMAINS
ARE HERE DEPOSITED

All of which is true; but the last sentence has caused some confusion to exist as to his final resting-place.

Well might it be written of Anthony Wayne as was written of a great explorer and inscribed on his tombstone,

"He was a man who cherished a task for its bigness and took to it with a fierce joy."

(1)

Lightning Source UK Ltd.
Milton Keynes UK
UKHW010245040119
334939UK00005B/76/P